HANNAH
SAVES THE
WORLD

a.m. luzzader

HANNAH SAVES THE WORLD

BOOK 1: MIDDLE GRADE MYSTERY FICTION

A.M. LUZZADER

ILLUSTRATED BY
CHADD VANZANTEN

KNOWLEDGE FOREST
PRESS

Published by Knowledge Forest Press
P.O. Box 6331
Logan, UT 84341

Ebook ISBN-13: 978-1-949078-21-3
Paperback ISBN-13: 978-1-949078-20-6

Cover design by Sleepy Fox Studio

Developmental and Copy Editing by Chadd VanZanten

Interior illustrations by Chadd VanZanten

To Melissa, thank you for puzzling it out with me and being a great sister

HIGH ABOVE PLANET EARTH, just at the edge of its atmosphere, a sleek and gleaming space cruiser loomed against the starry field of outer space, and on the command deck of this cruiser, there stood two alien beings.

Some of the humans down on Earth had seen the space cruiser. The aliens had technology to conceal their spacecraft, but it wasn't foolproof, and in fact, the space cruiser had been spotted from Earth no fewer than fifty times that day. It was fully the size of the Empire State Building, and when the invisibility technology wasn't working right, this spacecraft was hard to miss. And so, all across the country, reports flooded in from people claiming to have spotted a glimmering U.F.O. (which, you surely know, stands for "unidentified flying object").

Mrs. Janet Jellycake of Bugscuffle, Tennessee, called the police and cried, "I think there's a chance that I might have possibly spotted a potential U.F.O., maybe! At least I think so!"

Mr. Hank Highjinks of Grover's Mill, New Jersey, called the Air Force and in a very stern voice said, "Planet Earth is under attack!"

Ms. Wilhelmina Wigglestone of Goose Pimple Junction, Virginia, sent a twenty-minute cell-phone video to her local TV station, but the footage was so shaky and out of focus, it looked more like two kids playing catch with a flashlight on a foggy night in a backyard a mile away.

Nothing much resulted from these reports. There are U.F.O. reports all the time, all across the world, even when there are no alien spacecraft visiting Earth. Very few authorities ever take them seriously.

Of course, the aliens in the space cruiser knew nothing about the reports. Then again, they didn't think of their spaceship as a U.F.O., either. They had no trouble identifying their own flying object. The aliens knew perfectly well what it was and whom it belonged to. It was an Intergalactic Space Traveler Model THX-1138, which was fondly named something that roughly translated into English as the

"Shiny Vessel that Travels so Smoothly from Star to Star."

Furthermore, the aliens on board the *Shiny Vessel that Travels so Smoothly from Star to Star* did not consider themselves "aliens." They referred to themselves by their names. The first was called Aaxtchu, which, when properly pronounced, sounds very much like a human sneeze. The other's name was Brian, which, as it happened, was pronounced more or less like we say it on Earth, with perhaps a slightly stronger emphasis on the "i" and a little less on the "n".

The point is, Aaxtchu and Brian didn't think of themselves as alien invaders. Instead, they thought of Earth as an alien planet, a place they happened to be visiting that day, and they considered all of Earth's humans, animals, and plants as alien lifeforms.

Compared to the humans down on Earth, Aaxtchu and Brian were very tall. Their arms and legs were long and slender. Their hands resembled that of Earthlings, except their fingers were quite elongated, and each fingertip looked as though it had a big black olive stuck on the end. Their skin was the color of moldy bread, and their eyes looked like enormous black teardrops.

Aaxtchu and Brian wore long intergalactic robes,

which dragged along the deck of the *Shiny Vessel that Travels so Smoothly from Star to Star*, picking up little bits of dust and litter. The robes were so long, Brian and Aaxtchu appeared to glide across the deck of the spaceship rather than walk.

The two aliens stood gazing at an enormous monitor, which to be honest was way too big to even be called a monitor. It covered one entire side of the spaceship and was nearly the size of an Earthling football field. And on this immense screen, Aaxtchu regarded our Earth with envious eyes.

He tapped one bulbous fingertip thoughtfully on his chin. He turned to Brian and said, "'Klaatu barada nikto Earth."

Brian replied with, *"Earth!* Bababa dalgh araghtak ammina rronn konn bronn tonn!"

This was the way they talked. Their language was very different from the languages spoken on Earth, and theirs sounded a bit like the noise of blowing bubbles in milk using a straw, or the sound of walking in thick, deep mud.

What Aaxtchu said was, "After visiting many planets, I have come to the conclusion that this is the best place for us to construct our vacation dwellings."

"Ah, yes," said Brian, *"Earth!* Perfect distance from the sun, and just a hop, skip, and a light-speed jump from our homeworld. Sounds groovy. Should we fly the *Shiny Vessel that Travels so Smoothly from Star to Star* down to the planet's surface and begin planning for construction?"

Aaxtchu nodded, but then something on the massive monitor caught his large, inky eye, and he grimaced (let's not even bother to describe what that looked like). He pointed at the monitor and said, "Alas, there is a problem!"

"What's up?" asked Brian.

"See! This planet's atmosphere contains oxygen!"

"Ah, that's too bad," said Brian, also grimacing (trust me, you don't want to know). "With all that oxygen, it'd be totally lethal for us to vacation here. Guess we should keep looking, huh?"

"Wait a minute," said Aaxtchu. (He didn't actually say, "Wait a *minute*," of course, because Aaxtchu and Brian had their own system of time-keeping, in which the closest thing to a "minute" was called a "chronoblip," but "wait a minute" was essentially what Aaxtchu meant.) "Wait a minute," he said, calling up more information on the vast monitor. "It appears that Earth's atmosphere is only *twenty-one percent* oxygen. That is a relatively small proportion. The rest is mostly nitrogen, with small amounts of

5

other assorted gasses, such as carbon dioxide and neon."

"Ooo, neon!" exclaimed Brian. "I love the smell of neon in the morning."

"Let us fetch the de-oxygenator!" said Aaxtchu, raising one long, black-olive-tipped finger into the air. "It will clear the entire atmosphere of the toxic oxygen, and then we may commence the building of our vacation retreat!"

"Hey, Aaxtchu," said Brian, gazing at the greens and blues of Earth, "without oxygen, won't the native lifeforms suffer? Maybe even, you know, *die*?"

"What's that you say?" asked Aaxtchu, arching a thing above his eye that passed for an eyebrow.

"I mean the Earthlings and plants and other organisms and stuff down on Earth. What if they need the oxygen to, you know, *live*?"

Aaxtchu gestured at the monitor again. "Their air is only twenty-one percent oxygen. They obviously don't need it too badly."

Brian wore an expression that would be difficult to describe in words, but it indicated that he was skeptical, doubtful.

Aaxtchu blinked a few times and then waved a hand at Brian. "Do not be so sentimental. They're only *Earthlings*. Why, only ten thousand chronospans ago, they weren't even *housebroken*. Direct the Vogon Constructor Fleet to Earth at once! I will personally install, configure, and activate the de-oxygenator to make this planet the perfect place for our friends and families to visit in the summer."

"Big planet," said Brian. "Where do you plan to put this gizmo?"

"According to my calculations," said Aaxtchu, "taking into account the prevailing winds, planetary rotation, density of the atmosphere, and oxygen content, the best possible spot would be here—"

He pointed his long, bulbous fingertip at the giant Earth projection and it zoomed in at a dizzying rate. Immediately, mountains and cities became visible, and trees and streets and houses, too, until it settled on one particular quiet little road, which led to a sleepy little town with rows of pretty trees and trimmed green grass and neat little homes with white picket fences.

And alongside this quiet little road, there stood a sign that read *Welcome to Cardwick.*

CHAPTER 2

IT WAS Saturday morning in the little town of Cardwick.

Like most Saturday mornings in Cardwick, the Miller family was at home, sitting at the breakfast table, and their doorbell was ringing and dinging like mad.

And like most Saturdays when the doorbell was ringing like mad at the Miller's home, all four members of the Miller family knew who was at the door, without getting up from the table, without even glancing at the doorbell-camera app.

Mrs. Maria Miller knew, Mr. Marly Miller knew, and their daughters, Mia and Miley Miller, also knew who was at the door.

"It's Hannah," they all said in unison.

If they'd looked at the doorbell-camera app, they'd have seen Hannah waiting on the front porch. Hannah wore bright blue lipstick, her hair was fluffed up to maximum fluff-factor, and her oversized, goggle-like sunglasses flashed in the sunlight. She'd just inflated her bubble gum into a wobbly sphere the size of a softball. All at once it burst, and a thin pink stretchy skin of gum flapped onto her nose and sunglasses.

Mia's appearance was slightly less outrageous. Her straight dark hair was cut into a short bob, and she wore simple round eyeglasses.

The two girls were best friends. Oddly, Mia herself was always a bit unclear about how this had happened. How had they become such close friends? It happened suddenly, Mia knew, a bit like getting caught in a sudden rain—one moment you're walking along happy and dry, and a few chronoblips later you're drenched.

Mia may not have remembered, but it happened like this: Hannah and her family had moved to Cardwick a couple of years earlier. On that very first day, Hannah got on her bike and rode through Mia's neighborhood. Soon she'd spotted Mia, who was reading a book on her front porch. Without warning,

Hannah had skidded to a stop in front of Mia's house, parked her bike in Mia's driveway, and then stood there giving Mia a big grin.

"Uh, hi?" said Mia.

"Hi," said Hannah, with a deep and respectful bow. "My name's Hannah. It's spelled the same way forward and backward. And *you* are my new best friend."

At first, Mia looked to her left and then her right, unsure who the strangely bold girl was speaking to.

"You," said Hannah, pointing and still grinning. "I'm talking to *you*. You're my new best friend!"

"Oh," replied Mia. It was all she could think of to say. One moment, Mia didn't even know anyone *named* Hannah, and a few minutes later, someone named Hannah was her best friend.

Truthfully, Mia was quite shy, and she was secretly pleased by Hannah's bold declaration. From that time forward, Mia joined Hannah on practically all of her madcap misadventures.

Mia got up from the breakfast table, leaving behind her half-eaten waffles. She went to the door and opened it, and there stood Hannah, picking bubble gum off her face and sunglasses. But before Mia could even say, "Hello," Hannah stepped past her and in another few moments was climbing the stairs to Mia's bedroom.

"We need to talk," said Hannah over one shoulder.

"Hannah," said Mia, "would you like to talk over some waffles?"

Hannah spun around on the stairs. "I'd love some waffles! I assume you have some Kansas City barbeque sauce?"

"Barbeque sauce?" said Mia.

"No, not just barbeque sauce," corrected Hannah. "*Kansas City* barbeque sauce. I prefer my waffles dripping with authentic Kansas City rib sauce."

"Uh, no, I don't think we have any of that," said Mia.

"Then I'm afraid I'll have to decline," said Hannah with a polite gesture. "But thank you. Maybe some other time." She turned and continued up the stairs.

Mia made a little shrug and bounded after her. By the time she caught up, Hannah had already taken off her sunglasses and was pacing around Mia's bedroom.

Hannah took a deep breath and let it out slowly. "You better sit down."

Mia sat on her bed.

"No," said Hannah. "On second thought, you better stand up after all. You sitting there makes me nervous."

Mia stood back up.

Hannah clasped her hands behind her back as she paced the room again.

"Mia," Hannah said. "We need to save the world."

"Save the world from what?" asked Mia.

"Yes," said Hannah. "Yes, exactly."

"What?"

"Right. Precisely."

"Right precisely what?"

"Have you saved the world before, Mia? Because you seem to have a really firm grasp on the situation."

"No, Hannah, I have no idea what you're talking about."

"Oh," said Hannah. Then she nodded and then shrugged. "Sorry. I hear that a lot. What I'm telling you is that before we save the world, we have to figure out what we're saving it from."

"Well," said Mia. "That actually makes sense, in a way. But how do you know the world needs saving?"

"Just a feeling I have," said Hannah.

Mia wasn't sure at all what Hannah meant, but she was willing to wait for Hannah to clarify—if that were even possible.

"There is some good news," said Hannah, plopping onto Mia's bed.

"What is it?" asked Mia.

Hannah continued. "This feeling I have that tells me the world must be saved also tells me that you and I can save it together."

"But save it from *what*?" Mia asked again.

"Yes, exactly," said Hannah, sitting up straight. "So you *do* understand. We must save the world, but before we decide the *how* and *when*, we have to figure out the *what* and *why*."

Mia shrugged. "Okay."

"So, you're in?"

"I don't have anything else planned this week."

"I expected a bit more enthusiasm from you. Don't you even care?"

Mia shrugged again. "Of course I care. If the world needs saving, I'm in favor of saving it," she said.

Hannah looked at her with bewilderment. "Look," she said, "I know I've taken us on some wild adventures, but this is the *big* one! This one's *real!*"

15

Mia thought about all of Hannah's other "adventures."

Like the time Hannah became convinced that Bigfoot was secretly living in Cardwick's mini-golf course. To flush him out, Hannah and Mia played twelve mini-golf games in a row. From morning to sunset, they searched the mini-golf course, peering into the windows of the Dutch windmill, snooping endlessly through the hedge maze, and spying on the front gates of the great plaster castle with its moat, and the drawbridge that went constantly up and down. Mia and Hannah both made several holes-in-one. Indeed, they'd become masters of the mini-golf course, both scoring well under par, but in the end all that they'd really discovered was that their allowance money was severely depleted and their noses and cheeks were badly sunburned.

And then there was the time Hannah started an online video channel to share all of her conspiracy theories. They made videos about Hannah's broccoli conspiracy, in which Hannah theorized that boiled broccoli was a parasite that was trying to take over the cafeteria at school. "Say no to broccoli, and say yes to liberty!" cried Hannah. They'd made another video about the evils of homework. "Studies show it doesn't make you any smarter!" declared Hannah while gazing into the camera lens, "Which means it must make you stupider!" In the end, the online video channel received only a handful of views, mostly from Mia and Hannah's parents and a few lunch ladies, and the channel was quietly taken offline.

If Mia were being honest, she was more than a little skeptical about Hannah's latest caper. She wasn't sure if the world really needed saving, and if it did, Mia was unsure that she and Hannah could save it—not by themselves, anyway.

When Mia didn't answer right away, Hannah sat back up. "Think of it, Mia. We'll be heroes. They'll throw parades for us. People will name their *babies* after us. But more than that, we'll be saving humanity as we know it."

Mia really did not have anything else to do. Her homework was finished and her chores were done. If Hannah had a plan for them, she was game. Mia's glasses had slid down her nose, and she pushed them back up with her finger. "All right," said Mia. "Let's do it. Let's save the world."

But just then Mrs. Miller poked her head into Mia's bedroom. "Mia, it's almost time for your piano lessons."

"Oh, yeah," Mia murmured to herself, "I have *almost* nothing else to do."

Hannah stood up. "Mrs. Miller! Mia and I need to go save the world."

"Don't we all," said Mrs. Miller. "But the world will have to wait until after Mia's lessons."

After Mrs. Miller left, Mia shrugged and said, "I guess you better go home."

"Mia," said Hannah. "Look at me. This is very serious."

"I know," said Mia, "but why don't you start thinking of a plan on your own, and I'll think about it on my way to piano lessons, and we'll circle up later to compare notes."

To Mia's surprise, Hannah's face lit up. "That's a brilliant idea!" she exclaimed. "Dual independent collaborative brainstorming is just what this crisis needs."

"Sounds good," said Mia, as she walked Hannah out of her room and toward their front door.

Mia opened the door, but Hannah paused in the doorway and lifted up her sunglasses. "And don't be scared, Mia. We can do this. I believe in us."

Mia nodded. Even with all of Hannah's dramatics and over-the-top ideas, she was a lot of fun, and even if it was just for pretend, it might be really interesting to try to save the world.

"Let me know what you come up with," said Mia.

"Will do," said Hannah. She flipped her hair over her shoulder, got on her bike, and rode away.

CHAPTER 3

THE NEXT MORNING, Hannah was back, ringing the Millers' doorbell for all it was worth.

"Mia, Hannah is here," yelled Miley, Mia's younger sister.

Again, nobody had bothered looking outside to confirm it was Hannah. The time of day and Hannah's frantically persistent *ding-dong-ding-dong-ding*ing were the only clues anyone needed to figure out who it might be.

Mia went to the front door and opened it.

"Hello, Hannah," she said.

That morning, in addition to her over-sized sunglasses and signature blue lipstick, Hannah wore a long pink feather boa around her shoulders, and on her head sat a tall purple top hat she'd won at a carnival. The hat was balanced precariously on Hannah's massive shock of crimped hair. The countless feathers of the boa waved softly but flamboyantly.

Hannah removed her big sunglasses with a dramatic flourish and cried, "Mia! Why are you dressed like *that*? I mean, I like it. It's quite a pretty dress. And it's nice to see you taking our adventures seriously, for a change, but this outfit doesn't seem right for saving the world. It looks more like church clothes."

"It's Sunday," groaned Mia. "These *are* my church clothes. Why are *you* dressed like *that*?"

"What do you mean?" asked Hannah.

Mia pointed at the tall purple top hat. Then she picked up one end of Hannah's feather boa and waggled it for a moment. The feathers trembled in the morning air. Mia let the feather boa drop.

"Oh, *this*," said Hannah sweeping the end of the feather boa back around her neck. "It's in case I need a disguise. On a job like this, you never know when you might need to go under-cover and blend in."

"I see," said Mia.

"Well, let's not waste any more time," said Hannah. "Grab your bike, and let's hit the trail."

"I told you," Mia replied. "Today is Sunday. We're headed to church. I can't play."

Hannah dragged her hands down the side of her

21

face. "What is it with you never having time to save the world? Don't you *like* the world? Don't you think the world is, like, *important?*"

Mia shrugged. "Sorry, Hannah. My parents won't let me play on Sunday."

A shocked expression spread over Hannah's face. "Mia! This is not *play!* This is *serious* business. *Very* serious business! Can't you file for an exception? An exclusion? An exemption?"

But Mia didn't have to file anything because just then Mrs. Miller came to the front door and said, "Hello, Hannah. I love your outfit."

Hannah adjusted her feather boa and said, "Thank you, Mrs. Miller. Would it be possible for Mia to apply for some kind of special easement today? We have a lot of really important business to attend to!"

Mrs. Miller gave Hannah a wry grin and said, "No, I'm afraid not, Hannah. But it was sure nice seeing you. *Again.*"

"Okay, all right," mumbled Hannah. She looked dejected for a moment, but in another instant, she stood up straight, pointed at Mia, and said, "I want at least five ideas from you about what we're going to save the world from, Mia. Got it? And I want them on my desk by tomorrow morning!"

"I'll see what I can do," said Mia. "Maybe you can conduct some reconnaissance on your own today—your disguise will keep you concealed much better than my church clothes. Unless you're going to do reconnaissance at a church, I guess."

"That's very true," said Hannah. "With this ensemble, I'll be practically invisible. But you realize working undercover solo is much more dangerous, right? I'll be taking some huge risks."

Mia grabbed her friend's hand and said, "I believe in you. Be safe and wear your disguise. Don't blow your own cover."

"Will do," said Hannah putting on a serious face. Then she bowed and said, "Until tomorrow, then."

Mia likewise bowed and said, "Until tomorrow."

CHAPTER 4

Mia was on the school bus home when Hannah popped up over the back of the seat. She had a new pair of big sunglasses pushed back onto her hair. One lens was shaded blue and the other was red.

"Hannah," said Mia. "What are you doing? Why aren't you in your assigned seat?"

Hannah shot a suspicious look around the bus to see if anyone was listening. She didn't seem to notice Jared and Kyle, the two boys occupying the seat she was crouching in, and she didn't take notice of Melinda, who was sitting right next to Mia in her seat, nor did she seem to mind that they were literally surrounded by dozens of other bus-riding kids.

"Listen, Mia," said Hannah, "I've been waiting all day to talk to you."

"What do you mean? I saw you at school," said

25

Mia. "We have three classes together. We ate lunch together."

Hannah shook her head. "Couldn't talk there. Too many ears. I need to see you after we get off the bus. It's urgent."

"Oooh," said Mia. "Is it about saving the *you-know-what*?"

"Yes, saving the *world*, right, exactly," said Hannah. "I did some investigating on my own, as per our agreement, and I have found some pretty big clues."

"Clues about what?" asked Kyle.

"Shhh," Hannah hushed him. She turned back to Mia. "Let's rendezvous at the bus stop."

Mia had already planned to spend the afternoon with Hannah, and she'd been very much looking forward to Hannah's new caper, but in order to heighten the drama of the moment, Mia pretended to think about it for a few seconds, and then she said, "Okay."

"What's the big secret?" said Jared. "What's this meeting about?"

Hannah turned to him. "If we succeed," said Hannah to Jared and Kyle, "you'll never need to find out."

Jared and Kyle traded a puzzled look.

"And what if you fail?" asked Jared, his eyes wide with worry.

Hannah frowned and gazed wistfully into the air, her mismatched sunglass lenses glinting in the afternoon sun. "Let's not think about that right now."

When they arrived at their stop, Hannah and Mia got off the bus and moved away from the other kids.

"Well," Mia said. "What did you find out?"

Hannah looked around again. Jared and Kyle were standing close-by, trying to eavesdrop. She took Mia by the elbow and led her away.

"I think it's better if I show you," whispered Hannah to Mia. "We must evade all of these prying ears. Plus, we'll need our bikes."

Mia had to admit that her curiosity was piqued. They dropped off their backpacks at their home. Hannah grabbed her adventuring purse. Then they grabbed their bikes, put on their helmets, and rode out.

"So, where are we going?" Mia asked.

"Just follow me," said Hannah over her shoulder.

They rode along the streets of their neighborhood. The scent of lilacs from the Johnsons' front yard filled the air as the sun began coming down from the sky. Birds chirped melodiously. Little kids giggled and played in almost every direction.

"What a nice day," said Mia. She took a deep breath.

"Yes," said Hannah, "a perfect day to save the world."

"About that," said Mia. She was pedaling hard to keep up with Hannah, who was a little bit taller and much faster. "Are you still so certain that the world needs saving?"

"I told you, it's just a feeling I have," said Hannah, "but don't worry, Mia. The world's not going to end." Before Mia could reply, Hannah added, "We'll save it before it gets to that."

Hannah pedaled past the Post Office and then on past Kramer's, the only grocery store in town. The girls waved to people on the sidewalk and the people on the sidewalk waved back. After a few more blocks, Hannah turned toward Cardwick City Park. It was a lovely little place, with some nice open space, picnic tables, and a playground with swings and a slide.

"Are we going to the park?" asked Mia. "Can we go on the swings?"

But Hannah didn't need to reply, because as they rode into the park, Mia saw the trouble for herself.

Hannah and Mia both stopped biking.

"Doesn't this look like someone in the world is up to no good?" asked Hannah, gesturing with her hand.

The park's playground was barricaded by yellow tape emblazoned with the words *CAUTION: DO NOT ENTER.*

Inside the tape, the swings were torn down. The springs on the springy animals were broken—the lion and zebra were lying on the ground, and the hippo was nowhere to be found. Trash cans had been pushed over, and bits of paper and litter blew around in the breeze. The bike racks and picnic tables had been tipped over, too.

And as though that were not bad enough, everywhere they looked, there was garish graffiti in bright-blue and orange spray paint. On the tops of the picnic tables, on the walls of the restrooms, and even on the shiny surface of the slide, there were angrily scrawled spray-painted words.

Mia read some of it aloud. "'*White Timbers High is going to loose!*' What in the world does that mean?"

"They meant *lose*," said Hannah. "White Timbers High is going to *lose*. It's a common spelling error."

Even though Cardwick was a small town, small

29

enough that it only had one grocery store, it had two high schools. The school on the north side was Aspen High School. Their colors were blue and orange, and their mascot was a tiger. The school on the south side was White Timbers High School, whose colors were silver and purple, and their mascot was a knight.

"Lose what?" asked Mia.

Hannah opened up her purse and took out a pink plastic pipe. She put it in her mouth and began blowing bubbles. "Well, if I had to guess, the vandals are referring to the championship high school football game. It's this weekend."

Mia and Hannah were still in middle school, but in a small town that had two high schools, the competition between the two football teams was very exciting.

Mia shook her head. The other spray-painted messages had similar put-downs. "So someone from Aspen High did this?"

"To taunt the White Timbers footballers, yes," said Hannah. "Or so it would appear."

"Makes sense," said Mia. "This park is in the middle of town. And with a big championship game coming up, I could see one of the rival players doing this to try to undermine the confidence of the

White Timbers. Make them nervous before the game."

"Yes," said Hannah, as she began to pace. "The technical term for this is 'a psych-out'. According to my source, that's what the police think, too."

"Your *source*?" asked Mia.

"Yes," said Hannah, blowing on her bubble pipe. "In fact, my source says they've already charged someone with the crime."

Mia put her hands on her hips. "Who's your source?" she asked.

"Ben Billings," said Hannah.

"Your bus partner?"

Hannah nodded, blowing one gigantic bubble from the well of the pipe.

"How does he know?"

"Because he is best friends with Isaac Johnson," said Hannah, "and Ben was over at Isaac Johnson's house when the police came over to talk with Isaac's parents about Isaac's older brother, Mike. And then, later on, Isaac told Ben that Mike Johnson had gotten in trouble and was grounded forever and he'd been kicked off the Aspen High School football team and was probably going to be in big, big trouble with the police for all this vandalism. Ben told me on the bus today."

Mia sighed. "Wow, sounds like a lot of rumors are spreading. So, the police already know Mike Johnson did it?"

"The police *think* Mike did it, yes."

"You don't agree?"

"According to Ben, who was told by Isaac, who overheard it in his own house from police personnel, they knew Mike had done it because they found his letterman jacket here at the playground *and* he's the star quarterback for the Aspen High School team, so he has a motive for wanting to psych-out the students at White Timbers High School right before the big game."

"So, case closed," said Mia with a small shrug. "Not very nice of him, though, to ruin the playground this way. Especially because it's just for kids."

"Yes, the culprit seemed to know exactly what to do to cause the most upset."

"Culprit? You mean Mike?"

Hannah blew a few thoughtful pipe bubbles. Then she took the pipe out of her mouth and cradled it in her hand. "Mia, I think the police are wrong. We need to find out who really vandalized this park. It may not save the world, but I can't get rid of this gut feeling that the vandalism and the world-saving are somehow connected."

"Why do you think the police are wrong?"

"Four reasons," said Hannah.

She put the pipe back in her mouth and paced across the grass. Mia sat down to listen.

"Number one," said Hannah, holding up one finger. "As you've already noticed, the word *lose* was spelled incorrectly. And there are other very elementary mistakes and errors, such as, *Your all a bunch of wimps*. As you know, I am the sixth grade spelling-bee champion."

"Well, yes, but what difference does that make?"

"All winners of the sixth-grade spelling bee have their names inscribed on brass nameplates on the big spelling bee trophy, which is kept in the display case in the main hall. As a champion, I have read all of the names of the former champions." Here Hannah paused for effect. She blew a few more bubbles and turned her back to Mia.

Mia waited a few moments and then said, "And?"

"And!" said Hannah, spinning around dramatically. "It will interest you to know Mike Johnson was the spelling bee champion when *he* was in sixth grade."

"So?" said Mia.

"So, he would never have made such mistakes. He wouldn't confuse *loose* for *lose* or *your* for *you're*. We spelling bee champions simply cannot bring ourselves to misspell words if we can possibly help it. It goes against our nature."

"Well, maybe someone else was with him or maybe he was trying to throw the police off his track?"

"Which brings me to my second point," said Hannah, now holding up two fingers. "If I've learned anything from detective novels, it's that the guilty party is never who you think it is at first. The letterman jacket at the scene? Too obvious. The police are overlooking something, I just know it."

"But this isn't a *book*, Hannah. This is real life. Things don't always work the way they work in detective novels."

"Third!" said Hannah, showing three fingers. "You know that my dog, Orson, escapes from our fenced yard sometimes, do you not?"

"Yeah, he spends more time outside the fence than inside," said Mia.

"Precisely," said Hannah. "Well, it may further interest you to know that Mike Johnson has helped us re-capture Orson on more than one occasion, and once he even saved Orson from being hit by a car! Mike is obviously a caring person who would never do something to ruin the fun of young children. It just doesn't jibe."

"You can like animals and still commit crimes," said Mia.

"And finally," said Hannah turning on her heels. "I have a very strong gut feeling that Mike is innocent. It was the same feeling I got when I knew we were supposed to save the world. If I know my gut, and I think I do, the police have got the wrong guy. This is called *intuition*, and it is very important in solving mysteries."

"So, what do we do?" asked Mia.

"If I have learned anything else from detective novels, it is that a criminal often returns to the scene of their crime. Maybe whoever did this is going to come back. We should do a stakeout to see if they do," said Hannah.

"How will we know who it is?" asked Mia.

"Oh, I'll know," said Hannah.

Hannah unzipped her adventuring purse again and tucked the bubble pipe inside. Then, she pulled out two compact mirrors.

"Here," said Hannah, pressing one of the mirrors into Mia's hand. "You go hide in the bushes over there, and I'll hide in the bushes over here, and if either one of us sees something suspicious, we'll signal each other."

Hannah demonstrated by catching the light of the sun with the mirror and angling it so that it flashed in Mia's face. Mia squinted and reflected the sun into Hannah's face, and for a few minutes the stakeout was reduced to a game of "sun tag."

"Okay, enough of that," said Hannah. "You hide over on that side of the park, and I'll hide on this side. If you see any suspicious characters, signal me. I'll signal you if I see anything."

"Why not just yell or wave?" asked Mia.

"And blow our cover? I don't think so. Now, hurry and hide. Hopefully, we won't be waiting too long."

Mia found a hiding place in the shrubs around the outside of the park. She sat down and tried to hide. It wasn't super comfortable. A branch kept sticking her in the ear. At least she was able to sit down and enjoy the nice day, but after a while Mia got really bored. Through the bushes she watched as more and more kids arrived at the park, saw the vandalism, and then left disappointed. It made her angry. The poor kids just wanted to play. Someone had been really selfish to have done this to the playground.

Even though it was the first week of November, it was still quite warm. The sun was shining right on Mia, and she found herself squinting against the bright light.

She frowned and left her hiding spot to sit in a shady place under a tree. She was starting to doubt Hannah knew what she was talking about. Saving the world? The police being wrong? It just didn't make any sense.

Mia turned her head in the direction of Hannah's hiding spot. To her surprise, she saw a series of flashes from Hannah's mirror.

Mia sat up in a panic. How long had Hannah been signaling her? She tried signaling back, but then jumped to her feet and ran toward Hannah, hoping that nothing had happened to her friend.

CHAPTER 5

THAT SAME DAY, Aaxtchu and Brian had gotten clearance to load the de-oxygenator into the landing craft, which sat in the hold of the *Shiny Vessel that Travels so Smoothly from Star to Star*. The landing craft was only about as large as an Earthling pick-up truck, much smaller than the *Shiny Vessel that Travels so Smoothly from Star to Star*. Aaxtchu got into his spacesuit, which was much more tightly fitted than the intergalactic robes he wore while on board the *Shiny Vessel that Travels so Smoothly from Star to Star*. Then, Aaxtchu climbed into the cockpit of the landing craft. When it was powered up, he saluted Brian and flew out of the airlock and down into Earth's atmosphere to find some place in Cardwick to install the de-oxygenator.

The location had to be in a wide-open space so

that it could easily suck up oxygen, but it had to be in a secluded place, too, somewhere the alien Earthlings wouldn't disturb it. The last thing Aaxtchu needed was for someone to tamper with his machine. If that happened, the machine might not be able to remove the oxygen from the atmosphere. And if *that* happened, then his people wouldn't be able to vacation on the planet. And if *that* happened, well, Aaxtchu thought he might just lose his mind. He'd been working for 304 Earth days without any kind of break. Aaxtchu tried to maintain a professional and business-like attitude, but if anyone needed a serious vacation, it was Aaxtchu.

As the landing craft sped down through the skies above Cardwick, Aaxtchu spotted a nice open area in the middle of what looked like a farm field.

Aaxtchu purred, "Weezer wookie," which in English means, "Yes, wonderful."

Just then, Brian called on the subspace intercom. "Doddler boddler boolla?" Brian asked.

"Zaphod beeblebrox toyo tata coma," replied Aaxtchu. "Bill bow bagg inz."

Brian brought his black-olive fingertips together and said, "Weezer wookie! Weezer!"

This conversation was essentially Brian asking, "Have you found a good spot for the de-oxygenator?"

39

And Aaxtchu replying, "Yes, I have located an area that meets all of the technical requirements. All the oxygen should be removed in just ten chrono-plops" (which was approximately twelve hours on Earth).

"Groovy," answered Brian. "Good job!"

Both of them were thinking of how nice it would be to be down on the Earth, which was the perfect distance from the sun, without all that nasty oxygen in the atmosphere.

Sure, the plants, animals, and humans might not like the lack of oxygen, but Brian himself hadn't had a vacation in 647 Earth days, so he was quite desperate to have someplace to relax, too. The consequences to the living things on Earth seemed unimportant. In any case, Brian gave Aaxtchu a salute. Aaxtchu responded the same way, and the projection zapped off.

All Aaxtchu had to do now was to land in the field, set up the machine, and start it up. His hands deftly maneuvered two joysticks to fly the ship over the town of Cardwick. He didn't worry about the humans spotting him. The cloaking technology usually worked well, but humans had often spotted their spacecrafts, and for some reason it had never been a problem before. Aaxtchu didn't know this, but sightings of spaceships on Earth were almost always mistaken for weather balloons or experimental military jets or even figments of the imagination. They were usually just called "U.F.O.s" and then forgotten about. No one ever did anything about them, other than to tell stories about them at parties, even if there was actual video footage (which was almost always jiggly and very blurry).

So, down Aaxtchu flew in the landing craft until he was skimming over the town of Cardwick. He glided just a little above the houses, schools, and tree-tops. He slowed down the landing craft as he approached the alfalfa field that so perfectly matched the technical specifications for operation of the de-oxygenator, so he did not notice that he happened to be flying directly above the Cardwick City Park.

However, just at that moment, there was an intense flash, an insanely bright glint, apparently a beam of misdirected sunlight, which blazed into Aaxtchu's large eyeballs. His eyes and pupils were much bigger than human eyes, of course, and as a result, they were much more sensitive to the reflection caused by the sun reflecting off, for example, a hand-held compact mirror. You've probably experienced blobs of color in your vision after you look at a bright light such as a camera flash or a headlamp aimed at your face. Well, just imagine if your eyes were roughly ten times larger! The blobs that Aaxtchu saw in his vision were enormous and vivid and awfully distracting. Almost completely blinded, Aaxtchu could only hope that he was steering in the right direction.

But he was not steering in the right direction. In fact, he was flying upside down and toward the ground at a high speed and dangerous angle. And that is when there was another flash of light from the ground, which was again angled right into his eyes.

The long, slender olive-tipped fingers of Aaxtchu's hands briefly came away from the controller joysticks to shade his face, and the landing craft rapidly lost its remaining altitude. First the landing craft struck a tree, then a telephone pole, and then an old TV antenna that Cardwick resident Marshal Minton had mounted on a high mast above his house to pick up Canadian hockey games on TV.

Aaxtchu's landing craft might have been all right after that, but no sooner had Aaxtchu blinked his vision back to normal when the landing craft crashed into a more or less immovable object: Mrs. Lemon's backyard garden shed.

Mɪᴀ ʀᴀɴ across the park and found Hannah sitting under her own shrub, where she was tilting her mirror toward the sun.

"Hannah," cried Mia. "What is it?"

Hannah stood up and slapped the dust and dead leaves from the seat of her pants.

"This stake-out is obviously moving too slowly," said Hannah. "We can't sit here all day doing nothing. We need to take *action*. Besides, this is really boring. I'm practically falling asleep here."

"Why didn't you just come get me, then?" asked Mia. "Why did you signal me with the mirror?"

Hannah shrugged. "Well, for one thing, I wanted to see if our signaling system worked, and I wanted to see if you were paying attention. It did, and you were. Good job. This is exactly the kind of dedication we need to save the world. Now if we could only figure out a way to do it faster and in a less-boring way."

"So, what do we do now?" Mia asked.

"I think we should look around and see if there are any clues that the police missed," said Hannah.

"And if there's not?" Mia asked.

"Then we'll go talk to Mike Johnson and see if he has an alibi."

"What's an alibi?"

"An alibi is something that proves you were somewhere else when a crime was committed. This crime was committed here, at the park, at a certain time. If Mike can prove he was somewhere else at the same time, like if he was with other people who can tell the police, then Mike would have an alibi. It's a form of proof that a suspect is innocent. If someone has a solid alibi, it's proof that they didn't commit the crime."

"When was the park vandalized?" Mia asked.

"Late Saturday evening. I saw it Sunday morning when I did my investigation work on my own," answered Hannah. "Here, give me your mirror."

Mia handed Hannah the mirror, and Hannah put both mirrors back in her purse. Then she produced a large magnifying glass. The lens was held in a brass hoop and was the size of a saucer. The handle was made of wood. Hannah held it up to her face.

"Sorry," said Hannah, her blinking eye looking warped and owl-like through the lens. "I only have one of these. But we can take turns. Now, let's look for clues!"

Hannah and Mia prowled through the park, taking turns with the magnifying glass. Mia wasn't sure what they were looking for, but it was fun to look at the magnified grasshoppers and tree bark and the blades of grass.

After a few minutes, Mia said, "There doesn't seem to be anything unusual around here."

"I don't see anything either," Hannah replied. "But that doesn't mean there isn't something there. We just need to look harder."

"But it could mean there *isn't* something there," said Mia.

"What?"

"Not seeing anything could mean that there isn't anything there to see."

"I don't understand," said Hannah.

Mia gestured at the playground. "You're assuming that there is something else for us to find, but if the police collected all the evidence, there wouldn't be anything else to find, right?"

"Okay," said Hannah hesitantly.

"This park isn't that big," said Mia. "And they apparently already found Mike's letterman jacket."

"Yes," said Hannah. "It has his name on the back of it. But if he really did it, there's no way he would have been foolish enough to leave behind a jacket that I assume is very valuable to him *and* has his name on it."

"Good point," Mia replied reluctantly.

"Ah-ha!" shouted Hannah.

Startled, Mia stepped back. "What is it?"

Hannah bent over with the magnifying glass at her eye, peering intently at something on the ground.

Mia bent down and looked, too, but she didn't need a magnifying glass to see what it was. "A candybar wrapper?" asked Mia.

"Not just any candybar," proclaimed Hannah. "A Ga-Ga Gooey Bar."

"I love those," said Mia.

"So do I," said Hannah. "Everybody loves Ga-Ga Gooey Bars. They're amazing. And look, this one was jumbo-sized."

"Okay, but what's this have to do with

anything?" asked Mia. "The trash cans were tipped over. There's garbage spilled everywhere."

Hannah handed her the magnifying glass. "Look *closely*," she said, passing the magnifying glass to Mia.

Mia took the glass, crouched down, and studied the candybar wrapper. To her surprise, it seemed that this Ga-Ga Gooey Bar wrapper might indeed be a clue. On the corner of the wrapper, where it had been ripped open, there were smudges of what looked like two colors of paint—orange and blue—the same colors that were sprayed all over the playground.

"Is this paint?" asked Mia, shifting the magnifying glass to see better.

"Precisely," said Hannah. "Whoever committed this vandalism probably stopped to eat this candybar and didn't realize they'd gotten paint on the wrapper!"

"Or the wrapper could have been here before and some paint just got on it," suggested Mia.

"Maybe," said Hannah. "It's good to keep an open mind during an investigation. In any case, we should collect this as evidence."

Hannah opened her purse again and removed a large plastic baggie with a zip-lock opening. She then produced a pair of tweezers and used them to pluck the candy wrapper from Mia's hand. After dropping the wrapper carefully into the plastic baggie, she placed the clue into her adventuring purse. She then zipped the purse shut and patted it.

"Alrighty then," said Hannah. "Let's go see Mike Johnson."

CHAPTER 7

AAXTCHU, a little rattled from his crash with Mrs. Lemon's well-built backyard garden shed, fumbled with the hatch release on the landing craft. After a few tries, he got it open and struggled out of the small spacecraft. Aaxtchu was wearing his spacesuit, which allowed him to tolerate the harsh oxygen in the Earth's environment, but his knees were a bit wobbly.

While a spaceship up in the air may have avoided the notice of Earthlings, a ship on the ground—not to mention a spaceship lodged in the roof of a large and formidable garden shed, would undoubtedly draw their attention. And the last thing Aaxtchu needed was unwanted attention. As mentioned earlier, what Aaxtchu really needed was a vacation, and the sooner he got the de-oxygenator set up and running, the sooner he'd get it.

"What's going on down there?" It was Brian's voice on the subspace intercom. "I'm seeing some warning lights up here. Is the landing craft malfunctioning?"

"No," answered Aaxtchu, "but my flight trajectory has been interrupted by unintended contact with a ground-based obstacle."

Brian thought about this and then said, "You mean you crashed?"

"If you must put it that way, yes, I have *crashed*. Are your sensors picking up any nearby lifeforms?"

"No," said Brian. "No one is nearby. How's the landing craft?"

"The landing craft does not appear to have sustained any serious damage," said Aaxtchu.

"Well, how's it look? Give me a damage report."

Aaxtchu examined the landing craft. "The outer protective coating of pigment has been marred," he said.

"You mean you scratched the paint job," replied Brian.

"Yes," answered Aaxtchu, still checking on the landing craft. "Also, it appears that the rearward-monitoring reflective device on the starboard side of the vessel is nowhere to be found."

"You mean the right rear-view mirror is gone."

"Correct," said Aaxtchu.

"Okay," said Brian. "Sounds like the damage was minimal."

The same could not be said about Mrs. Lemon's garden shed. It was still standing, mostly, but one wall was caved in, and the shed now had a small alien landing craft where most of the roof used to be. Shovels, garden tools, and broken flowerpots lay strewn across Mrs. Lemon's backyard.

But Aaxtchu didn't have time to worry about that. A partially demolished garden shed could not stand in the way of the planetary invasion of hundreds of vacationing aliens. It was a minor setback, Aaxtchu reasoned, one that he could easily handle.

All he had to do was to pull the craft off of the shed, and then he'd be able to start it up again and fly away without incident. This is a minor setback, Aaxtchu thought.

The landing craft was made of very light-weight alien materials, and so it was rather light. Aaxtchu should have had no problem dislodging it from Mrs.

Lemon's garden shed. But there was more to it than that. First of all, it was smashed into the roof of the shed, and it wasn't easy for Aaxtchu to climb up there, despite the fact that he was much taller than the average Earthling. Next, when Aaxtchu was finally able to climb to the roof of the shed, he found it was angled sharply and quite unstable, and he fell through it into the shed, which was filled with a confusion of rakes, fence posts, stacked-up flower pots, and an oily old lawnmower, not to mention cobwebs, dust, and several torn-open sacks of last year's garden manure. Soon Aaxtchu was banged up, dirty and smeared with stale cow manure.

"How's it going down there?" asked Brian over the subspace intercom. "Everything all right?"

"No," replied Aaxtchu testily. "Everything is far from *all right*. I have fallen into some strange tiny dwelling, which is not only dark but full of very inconvenient items!"

"My readings show that it is a garden shed," said Brian. "Better watch out, it will probably contain rakes and sharp tools and maybe even some spiders."

"Thank you for the bulletin," huffed Aaxtchu as he struggled to escape the shed and dust himself off.

Aaxtchu was weary and frustrated and covered

in a thin layer of light-purple sweat when he finally managed to pull the scratched-up landing craft off of Mrs. Lemon's garden shed.

"I am re-commencing operations," he said to Brian on the subspace intercom.

"You might want to hurry up," said Brian. "You don't want to be spotted by Earthlings."

Aaxtchu rolled his eyes. As senior officer, he should have assigned Brian to come down and install the de-oxygenator. But even though Aaxtchu was now covered in sweat and dust, he thought, he might as well finish the job. He was lifting the hatch and was about to climb into the landing craft, when he was startled by a strange noise. It sounded like numerous wheels and gears and a basketful of Earthling puppies thundering in his direction. When he turned to look, however, he saw that it was only two noisy Earthling girls giggling and chattering as they rode their bicycles down the street. Aaxtchu dove into a nearby hedge and called Brian on the subspace intercom.

"Lifeforms approaching!" he hissed. "Why didn't you tell me?"

"You didn't ask," Brian replied. "Don't worry. Sensors show it's just a couple Earthling kids on primitive, two-wheeled vehicles."

"Yes, but they're so loud," said Aaxtchu, peeking through the hedges. "And one of them has blue lips!"

"Probably all that oxygen in their atmosphere. It can't be good for them."

In only a few seconds, the two young Earthlings had whizzed past and were gone, the uproar of their laughter and bicycle tires fading down the road. Aaxtchu sighed deeply. He'd thought it was a close call, but everything was fine. It was time to get back on task. Move the ship. Install the de-oxygenator. And then vacation at last. Zingle, zong, zang.

Aaxtchu walked over to the spacecraft, relieved that the girls hadn't seen it. He lifted the handle on the hatch but to his surprise the door was locked.

"Hooteeny!" Aaxtchu exclaimed. He patted his spacesuit, trying to find the pocket where he had stowed the spacecraft's keys. But to his alarm, all his pockets were empty.

"Hooteeny," Aaxtchu repeated sadly. He must've dropped the keys in his attempt to hide from the girls or clambering out of Mrs. Lemon's garden shed, or dragging the landing craft off the roof of the shed. Aaxtchu looked around at Mrs. Lemon's spacious green lawn and the neatly trimmed hedges surrounding it. He looked at the flowerbeds and ornamental shrubs. The keys could be anywhere, thought Aaxtchu. And meanwhile, the humans could find him at any moment. Aaxtchu sighed in his planetary suit and his large ink-black eyes blinked slowly. Maybe this was going to be difficult after all.

CHAPTER 8

Mrs. Johnson answered her door to find Hannah and Mia standing outside.

"Hello, girls," said Mrs. Johnson.

"Hello, Mrs. Johnson," Hannah replied politely. "My name is Hannah. It's spelled the same way frontwards and backwards. This is Mia. Her name isn't a palindrome like mine, but if you turn it backwards, it spells 'aim,' which is kind of cool."

Mia nodded.

"I see," said Mrs. Johnson, trying to conceal her confusion. "What can I do for you?"

"We were wondering if Mike is home," said Hannah.

"Yes, he's here," said Mrs. Johnson, "but I'm afraid he's grounded right now, and can't have any visitors. Is Mike"—Mrs. Johnson wore a puzzled expression—"is he expecting you?"

Hannah and Mia looked at each other. They were surprised that Mrs. Johnson had thought two girls in middle school were there to hang out with her son, a star of the high school football team.

"No, probably not," said Hannah. "This isn't a social call. We're actually here doing a"—Hannah thought for a moment—"a research project. We have some questions for Mike."

"Oh, uh, well," stammered Mrs. Johnson, still puzzled, "in that case, let me go get him."

Mrs. Johnson invited the girls into the living room, then disappeared into the house to fetch Mike. After a few minutes, a very sad-looking Mike Johnson came into the living room. His blond hair was messy, as if he'd just gotten out of bed, and even though it was late in the afternoon, he was wearing rumpled sweats and mismatched socks.

"Hello," mumbled Mike, obviously unprepared for the sight of Mia and Hannah waiting to see him. If Mrs. Johnson was puzzled by the visit, Mike Johnson was positively baffled.

Hannah approached Mike and held out her hand. Mike shook it slowly, as though in disbelief.

Hannah knew Mike, not only because of the time he helped her with Orson, but also because he had been the sixth grade spelling bee champion a few years before. Mia knew who Mike was because he was the star quarterback of the Aspen High School football team and often appeared in the newspaper and sat in the back of a convertible during the high school homecoming parades. But it was quite obvious that Mike didn't recognize either Hannah or Mia.

"Mike, I'm Hannah. You might remember me because my name is a palindrome and you helped rescue my dog a few times."

Mike mumbled.

"Doesn't matter," said Hannah. "I'm pretty sure you'll remember me after this. This is my assistant— er, my friend—Mia."

Mia raised her hand and said, "That's *aim*, if you spell it backwards, by the way."

Hannah nodded, then continued. "We have come to question you about the vandalism at the playground."

"Huh?" said Mike, scratching his head.

"We want to talk to you about the playground," Hannah said.

"Is this for your school paper or something?

Listen, I didn't do it, okay? And you better not be writing up something untrue about me. It's bad enough that I was grounded, but now I've been suspended from playing in the championship game, when I had nothing to do with it."

"We are not employed by the media. We are private, independent investigators," said Hannah.

"Right," said Mia. "We just want to make sure that the right person is held responsible."

Mike shook his head. "I've already talked to the police." He stood to go.

"Wait," Hannah said. "We're not sure the police got it right! That's why we're looking into it."

Mike sat back down. "You two?" he asked incredulously. "You're investigating the vandalism?"

"Yes, we two," said Hannah.

"No offense," said Mike with a shrug, "but I don't think two middle-schoolers are going to make much of a difference."

Both Mia and Hannah were hurt by the comment, but they tried not to show it.

"Maybe not," said Hannah, "but right now we might be the only friends you've got."

"What do you mean?" asked Mike.

"The police have already made their decision, right?" Hannah asked.

"Yeah, I have to appear in community court next week."

"And you're grounded, so you can't do any investigation work on your own, right?" Hannah continued.

"I guess not."

"And most people assume you are guilty, so no one else is going to help you."

At this, Mike frowned and folded his arms.

"You want to play in the championship game, don't you?" asked Hannah.

"Well, I don't know who did it, if that's what you're here to ask," said Mike. "All I know is, it wasn't me."

"Great," said Hannah. "We just want to ask a few questions and then we'll be on our way." She unzipped her purse and pulled out a miniature notepad and pencil and handed them to Mia. "Take notes, please."

Mia flipped open the cover of the notepad. "Ready," she said.

"Okay, first question," said Hannah. "Where were you Saturday evening when the vandalism took place? Do you have an alibi?"

Mike sighed deeply. "That's part of the problem. I was all alone. I was feeling stressed about the big game, so I decided to go for a walk by myself. I was gone for about an hour, but I didn't go anywhere near that park. I swear!"

"Did anyone see you?" asked Hannah. "Is there anyone who can corroborate your statement?"

"No." Mike shook his head. "I didn't see anyone. If I had I would have gone to them already."

Hannah turned to Mia and pointed at the notepad. "Write down: *no alibi*," she said.

Mia complied.

"Okay, next question," Hannah said, looking back up to Mike. "Why was your jacket at the scene?"

"Who told you that?" Mike asked.

"I have my sources," said Hannah.

Mike looked even more agitated. "I lost the jacket three or four weeks ago. I think I might have left it at practice. Or maybe somebody swiped it. I've been looking for it this whole time."

Hannah turned again to Mia. "Write the word *framed* and put a question mark."

"Yeah," said Mike. "That's it! I was framed."

"Do you have any idea who would have done it?" asked Hannah.

Mike shook his head again. "Nah. But I can tell you it wasn't any of the guys on our football team.

There's no way they would have risked not getting to play in the final game. We've all been on our best behavior. The coaches warned us in advance not to get in any trouble."

"I see," said Hannah. And to Mia, she said, "Write down: *big game*."

"So, there's a big rivalry between your team and the other school's team?" Hannah asked.

"Well that's no secret," said Mike. "Why does such a small town need two high schools, anyway?"

"It is a mystery," said Mia.

"Okay, last question," said Hannah. Here she paused for dramatic effect, then she pointed at Mike suddenly and asked, "What's your favorite candybar?"

"What's that got to do with anything?" Mike asked, raising an eyebrow.

"Just answer the question, please," said Hannah.

"Ga-Ga Gooey Bars. No question. I love 'em. Can't get enough of them," said Mike.

Hannah and Mia exchanged glances. Mia wrote *Ga-Ga Gooey Bars* in the notebook.

"Very interesting, Mr. Johnson," said Hannah. She gave Mike a long thorough look, and then she abruptly stood up. "Thank you for your time," said

Hannah curtly. "We'll let you know if we make any discoveries or hear of any new revelations."

"Wait," said Mike. "Aren't you going to tell me what's going on? Who did it? Who set me up?"

"It's still an open investigation," said Hannah with a dramatic gesture. "Come on, Mia, we must go."

The girls walked down the porch steps, and then Mia glanced back to see if Mike had shut the door. When she had confirmed that he had, she turned to Hannah. "Ga-Ga Gooey Bars? No alibi? A big rivalry with the other school? Hannah, he's guilty!"

"So it seems," said Hannah coolly. She rummaged in her adventuring purse and drew out the bubble pipe. A small swarm of bubbles floated out over Mike Johnson's front yard. "However," added Hannah, "things are not always as they appear. Now come! We must gather more information."

"How can we do that?" asked Mia.

"The paint had to come from somewhere. Let's go to the store and see if we can find any tips there," said Hannah.

"Sounds good," said Mia.

"Okay, but first I need to take Orson on a walk.

You know how he gets when he's been in the house all day."

"Will we have time for that?" asked Mia.

"We'll just go around the block," said Hannah. "It won't take too long."

CHAPTER 9

ON HIS HANDS AND KNEES, Aaxtchu crawled around Mrs. Lemon's neatly trimmed grass, looking for the keys to the landing craft while trying to remain out of sight. The cloaking technology for the landing craft was functioning, mostly, which meant that passersby probably could not see the alien vessel there in Mrs. Lemon's yard, but Aaxtchu still had to hide from the Earthlings who walked past with their dogs and baby strollers. The face screen of his spacesuit kept fogging up and obstructing his vision, and he was feeling quite cross. This was supposed to be an easy operation, but he'd had nothing but difficulties.

He still hadn't found the key. He'd called Brian to bring down the spare key, but Brian had foolishly left the spare key inside the landing craft. So, what if

Aaxtchu never found the lost key? The landing craft was constructed of mithril-adamantium alloy—it was practically indestructible. And the nearest certified intergalactic locksmith was hundreds of lightyears away. He'd never be able to get in without that key.

Aaxtchu went on searching feverishly, determined to set up the confounded de-oxygenator, get off planet Earth, and return to his base to start the vacation home construction project. Ignoring the pain in his knees and elbows, he crawled through the grass and mud, not caring about the sticks and rocks that hurt his boney knees and spindly fingers. He looked for what seemed like hours, and he was about to give up when his bulbous fingertips ran across something small and jangly and metallic.

"Weezer wookie!" Aaxtchu exclaimed, snatching up the key and holding it up to the light. He immediately felt more at ease. Maybe things would turn out all right after all.

With a great sigh of relief that once again fogged up the face screen of his planetary suit, Aaxtchu stood up and proceeded to the landing craft. However, just then, something very fast and squirrelly struck him in the knees. Some kind of canvas cable wrapped around his legs, and Aaxtchu was knocked onto his back.

Aaxtchu couldn't see what this thing was, but it jumped onto his chest and began licking the face screen of his planetary suit. Not only was it fogged from the inside, but now the outside was covered with foreign alien Earth slobber!

Horrified and assuming he was under attack by some hostile Earth organism, Aaxtchu screamed, "Mixer miyageee!"

Then Aaxtchu heard an Earthling voice crying "Orson! Orson! Orson, you silly dog, get back here!"

Aaxtchu pushed whatever it was off of him and dove back into the bushes to hide.

It was the loud little Earthling girl with the unfortunate blue lips! She grabbed the small but vicious creature's leash and chided, "Why do you always run away from me? You're probably getting into trouble that I don't even know about!"

When the Earthling and the hyperactive Earth beast had left Mrs. Lemon's backyard, and Aaxtchu heard the girls trailing off into the distance, he dared to step back out of the bushes.

"Lolapollooza," Aaxtchu sighed. "That was close."

There'd been too many close calls. He needed to get this job done and get out of there. He needed his vacation. He walked back to the ship. But wait. Where was the key?

Aaxtchu jumped from one foot to the other. "Ood, abbad abbay," he cried, which was to say, "No, no, no!"

He had dropped the key, again.

Aaxtchu's eyes crossed over Mrs. Lemon's expansive backyard of lush green grass again. If his species had been the crying type, Aaxtchu would have been crying then.

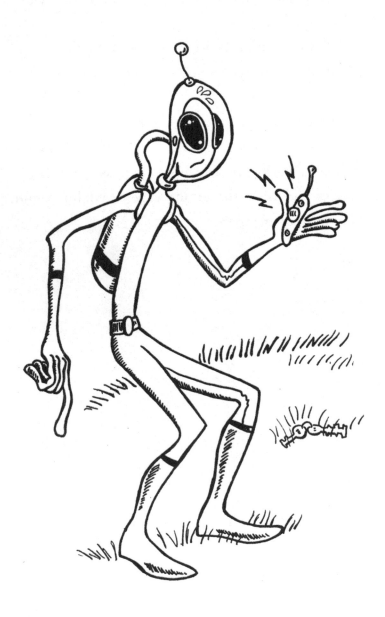

CHAPTER 10

HANNAH AND MIA leaned their bikes on the brick wall alongside the Kramer family grocery store. They didn't lock them up. Despite the recent vandalism of the city park, they didn't worry about someone stealing their bikes. After all, even though the town had two high schools, it was small and friendly, and everyone knew each other. Theft wasn't a big problem in Cardwick—or so they thought.

"So, what exactly are we looking for now?" Mia asked as they walked toward the glass front doors of the entrance.

"Clues," said Hannah.

"What kind of clues?" asked Mia.

"Well, first of all, have you ever considered just how *weird* the word 'clues' is? It's one of the most bizarre words in the entire English language, if it even *is* English. Clue. Clues. Clued. It's just—a strange word."

"Hm, yeah, I suppose you're right, Hannah. Clued, clues, cluuuue. So, what kind of clues will we find here?"

"That's the other unique thing about clues, Mia. You don't know what they are until you find them. If I knew what kind of clues were going to be lying around in Kramer's store, we wouldn't really need to be here."

"I guess you're right about that, too," said Mia.

"But we do want to check on Kramer's selection of spray paint, to see if they have the same colors that were used at the scene of the city park graffiti."

Kramer's was the only store in Cardwick that carried hardware items like spray paint. In the paint section, Hannah and Mia surveyed the rainbow-like rows of spray paint lined up on the shelves.

"Hey, look," said Mia. "This looks like the blue paint that was used." She pointed to a can of bright blue spray paint.

"And here's the orange," said Hannah, pointing to a can on the other side of the color spectrum. She searched through her purse and produced the evidence bag with the candy wrapper in it. "Yep," she said, comparing the color on the wrapper to the spray paint cans, "these are the same colors."

"Okay, so now what?" Mia asked.

"I wonder if this is where the paint came from," said Hannah studying the cans.

"The colors look like exact matches," said Mia. "Besides, where else would they get paint from?"

"I don't know, but look—it doesn't seem like any cans are missing on these shelves. They're all full."

Mia grabbed a blue spray paint can and said, "Wait, check this out!"

Mia and Hannah bent to look, and they saw empty space—enough for at least two cans of spray paint.

"Ah ha!" said Hannah. "I think the graffiti spray paint really *did* come from this store!"

"Why?" asked Mia.

"Retail stores always try to keep their products at the front of the shelf," said Mia. "So, it isn't surprising that there were cans right up front, but what *is* surprising is that someone moved up just one blue can and one orange can, but left all this space behind them. It's almost like someone was trying to hide the fact that a few cans were missing."

"Yeah," said Mia. "It's fishy."

"Let's go ask Mrs. Kramer if she knows anything

about it," said Hannah, collecting one can of each of the colors.

The two girls found Mrs. Kramer at the front of the store working at the cash register.

"Hi, Mrs. Kramer," said Hannah.

"Hello, Hannah! Hi, Mia!" Mrs. Kramer answered. "Thank you for stopping by. May I help you with anything?"

Mia and Hannah liked Mrs. Kramer. Sometimes when they bought penny candy, she'd give them a few pieces for free.

"Yes," said Hannah, holding up the two spray paint cans. "Do you know if anyone bought these colors recently?"

"You're asking because of the vandalism at the playground, aren't you?" said Mrs. Kramer with a clever smile.

"Yes," said Hannah. "We're hoping to find the responsible party."

"Oh, really?" said Mrs. Kramer. "I heard they found the culprit. One of the football players on the Aspen High School team."

"Oh, so the paint *was* purchased here?" Hannah asked again.

"Goodness, no. I don't sell much spray paint, and I'd

remember if anyone had bought some, but I checked my inventory and receipts anyhow, and no one has bought any of those two colors in ages," said Mrs. Kramer.

Hannah and Mia exchanged glances.

"But did you know there are cans missing from your shelves?" asked Hannah. "A couple cans of each of the colors used in the incident. All the other rows are full."

"That can't be," said Mrs. Kramer. "I checked the inventory and receipts myself!"

"Come look," said Mia.

Mrs. Kramer called on one of her other employees to take over at the register and then she joined the girls back at the paint aisle.

Mrs. Kramer frowned. "They're missing, all right. These shelves should be full, according to my inventory records. So, the spray paint used in the vandalism was stolen! I suppose I should inform the police. What a disappointment that someone in Cardwick would sink so low. Now I'll really be rooting for the White Timbers!"

"We're real sorry, Mrs. Kramer," said Mia.

"Oh, it's not your fault," said Mrs. Kramer with a shrug. "But it is upsetting, isn't it? I don't often go to the sporting games, but I will this time, and I'll be cheering loud and proud for the White Timbers football team!"

"So, this graffiti incident has got you really cheering for White Timbers, eh?" Hannah asked as she set the spray paint cans back on the shelves.

"Oh, yes!" said Mrs. Kramer. "I hope Aspen High gets royally trounced! Those rascals!"

"Interesting," said Hannah. "Say, Mrs. Kramer, on another topic, do you have any Ga-Ga Gooey Bars?"

"Seems like everyone who comes into the store asks me that," said Mrs. Kramer. "They're delicious, aren't they?"

"They seem to be very popular," said Mia.

"That's the problem," said Mrs. Kramer. "They're *too* popular! The candy company who manufactures them can't keep up with demand. We've been sold out since way before Halloween. In fact, the candy company sent me just one case for Halloween sales, and Mr. Norris bought that whole case the same day it arrived."

"Mr. Norris bought your *whole case* of Ga-Ga Gooey Bars?" Hannah asked.

"He sure did. Can you believe it? They were jumbo-sized, too. Fifty candybars!" said Mrs. Kramer.

"Wow," said Mia. "Did he say what he was going to do with all those Ga-Ga Gooey Bars?"

"I wasn't here at the time," said Mrs. Kramer. "Scott, one of my clerks, told me about it. You know Scott Scamperson?"

"No," said Hannah.

"He goes to White Timbers High School, I think," said Mia. "Plays on the football team."

"Yes," said Mrs. Kramer. "He was here when Mr. Norris bought all the Ga-Ga Gooey Bars. Scott said Mr. Norris was going to hand out all those big candy-bars on Halloween!"

"Really?" asked Hannah.

"Yes," Mrs. Kramer replied.

"Wow! Better write that down," Hannah said to Mia. "Full jumbo-sized Ga-Ga Gooey Bars on Halloween!"

"Roger that," Mia made a note in the evidence notebook.

"Well, girls, I better get back to the register," said Mrs. Kramer. "I'm sorry that I don't have any Ga-Ga Gooey Bars, but I have some Cherry Cha-Cha Bing Bars if you want to try those."

"Maybe," said Hannah. "I'd like to look around for a bit longer."

"Okay, let me know if you need anything," said

Mrs. Kramer, and then she returned to the front of the store.

"I really do want to look around while I think," Hannah told Mia, and they began walking up and down the aisles.

"So, Mike stole the paint," said Mia. "It makes sense. If he had purchased it, Mrs. Kramer would remember, and she'd have told the police."

"We don't know that Mike stole it," said Hannah. "We only know that it *was* stolen. But if Mike isn't guilty, the person who *did* steal it probably did for the reason that you said—to protect their identity. If they had bought the paint, the person at the register probably would have remembered it."

"So, it might have been Mike, but it might have been someone else," said Mia.

"Right," said Hannah. "The stolen spray paint is a fine clue, but we still need more information."

Mia was still writing down a few notes when Hannah stopped abruptly to examine a can sitting on one of the grocery shelves.

"Mmm," purred Hannah. "*Miss Mongo's Mystery Meat: Mystifyingly Mouthwatering Muscly Morsels.*"

Mia wrinkled her nose.

"I think I'll eat this for a light, after-school snack," said Hannah.

"You can't be serious."

Hannah shrugged. "The can says it's mouthwatering! And it says it's now made with extra gristle. I am getting hungry, and when I'm hungry, I don't think straight. Ooh, maybe I could fry it up with some pineapple and ketchup."

Mia was aware of Hannah's peculiar culinary preferences. Practically everyone knew that Hannah ate peanut butter and pickle sandwiches. She put grape jelly on mashed potatoes. And she liked to sprinkle garlic salt on her chocolate ice cream. But this combination was the worst yet.

"Eww," said Mia. "Hannah, that sounds gross. Pineapple, ketchup, and canned mystery meat? I think it's true—you're definitely not thinking straight."

"How do you think chefs come up with new recipes?" said Hannah, collecting her ingredients. "They have to experiment. This could end up tasting really yummy. Let's try it."

Hannah bought the strange canned meat, the pineapple, and a bottle of ketchup. Mia bought some Cherry Cha-Cha Bing Bars and a package of bubblegum.

79

"I'm getting super hungry," said Hannah. "Let's go to my house and I'll cook up my new dish for my after-school snack break. Like I said, my thinking process gets a little weird when I'm hungry."

"Right, but only when you're hungry, huh?" said Mia sarcastically.

They left the store and got on their bikes, but before they set out, Hannah said, "Hold on. I want to see if they're saying anything about the park incident on the local news radio station." She reached into her purse and brought out a small radio.

"Is there anything you *don't* have in that purse?" asked Mia.

Mia thought the radio was rather small, but then Hannah pulled out the antenna—and she kept pulling it out. The antenna just kept coming out and coming out—it was already over seven feet long, and Hannah wasn't done extending it.

"My dad and I used a soldering iron to replace this radio's antenna with one from an army-surplus walkie-talkie. I can pick up radio stations from all over the world with this thing," explained Hannah.

"You never cease to amaze me," said Mia.

When the antenna was fully extended, it was ten feet long. Hannah used a small velcro strap to fasten the radio to the handlebars of her bike so that she could listen to it while she was riding. Then she switched the radio on and the two girls started out down the street on their bikes.

Hannah turned the speaker volume up. "Okay, let's see what they're saying on the news."

Oddly, what played through the radio's speaker was definitely not the local radio news. In fact, the sound was unlike any human voice or anything the two girls had ever heard. It was a bubbling, burbling, blubbery sound.

"That's weird," said Hannah, swiveling the antenna around. "Do you hear that, Mia? Sounds like someone taking a bath in a tub full of pudding."

Mia said, "Yeah, or maybe like the sound of blowing bubbles in milk using a straw, or the sound of walking in deep, thick mud."

Hannah adjusted the tuning knob, but the weird blubbering bubbly noises only got worse. She frowned at the radio and said, "I've never had any trouble with this radio. I'll have to crack it open when I get home and give it a full diagnostic check."

Neither of the two girls noticed what was going on in the sky, but just fifty feet above the street where Mia and Hannah rode their bikes, a small alien spacecraft and its pilot were experiencing an extreme electronic emergency.

CHAPTER 11

AT LAST AAXTCHU was back in business. He'd found the keys in Mrs. Lemon's flowerbed. Now he was back in the landing craft and the landing craft was back in the air. Aaxtchu worked the controls roughly, taking out his frustration on the instrument panel. This project should have been finished several chronoplops ago, but Aaxtchu had yet to really get started. And so he was in a grumpy mood. No wonder he needed a vacation! Every simple mission he was sent on seemed to turn into a major pain in the scrabdabbler.

Nevertheless, the small landing craft soared through the sky and was fully cloaked and invisible. As Aaxtchu looked idly down from his place in the cockpit, he noticed some movement down on the surface—it was the same two little Earthlings who had made him lose his keys, not once but twice. They were still riding their primitive two-wheeled contraptions, no doubt looking for more trouble to cause. Aaxtchu thought it would probably be best to avoid these two, but he thought it might be wise to transmit a bulletin to Brian over the subspace intercom. He pressed a few buttons on his instrument panel.

"This is Aaxtchu calling Brian. Come in, Brian."

There was no answer.

"Brian!" Aaxtchu repeated in an irritated tone. He glanced at the street below to ensure that the two troublesome Earthling lifeforms were still in sight. "Brian! Answer, please. This is Aaxtchu down on the Earth's surface."

"Oh, hey there, Aaxtchu. What's up?"

"I've been trying to reach you," growled Aaxtchu. "Why didn't you answer?"

"Relax, Aax," replied Brian. "I was just cataloging the Earth's planetary electronic communication network. They call it 'The Internet.' Kind of a boring name, if you ask me. It seems to be mostly pictures of cats so far. Anyway, what can I do for you?"

"I want to submit a bulletin. There are two very troublesome and hostile Earthlings down here. Every time I turn around, they somehow manage to thwart my purposes!"

"They manage to *what* your *whats?*"

"They thwart my purposes! They've thwarted me not once but twice!"

Aaxtchu didn't actually say "thwarted my purposes," of course. He said it in his own language, which sounded more like "truffala thneed gazump."

"What do you mean by—thuh-war-ted?" asked Brian. "What's thwarted?"

"They have interfered with my tasks! They've upset my objectives!"

"Oh, you mean they've tripped you up," said Brian. "They're getting in your way."

"Yes, yes!"

"Okay, why didn't you just say so?" said Brian. "Okay. I'll make a log entry of them. What do these hostile lifeforms look like?"

"I shall send you a subspace video feed of them," said Aaxtchu. "Just let me maneuver a little closer—"

Just then, a shower of sparks erupted from Aaxtchu's instrument panel.

"Buckaroo banzai!" cried Aaxtchu, which in his language was an exclamation used to express surprise and alarm, but it also wasn't a very polite thing to say, so it's meaning won't be translated here.

"Aaxy, you know we're not supposed to use that kind of language on the subspace intercom," scolded Brian. "My sensors are showing that your communications are experiencing some interference from the planet's surface. Do you see any large communication devices around there? If so, you should probably steer clear of them."

When Aaxtchu looked out of the windows of the landing craft, he saw it! The little Earthling with the blue lips had deployed some kind of mobile anti-spacecraft device. It was a small gadget strapped to the handlebars of her riding contraption, and extending from it was a long shiny probe, which was picking up Aaxtchu's subspace transmissions and causing a disruptive feedback. When Aaxtchu attempted to turn right, the landing craft went left. When he tried to climb, the landing craft lost altitude. He struggled to control the spacecraft, whizzing this way and that, narrowly dodging trees and housetops and telephone poles.

"These Earthlings are even more dangerous that I thought!" cried Aaxtchu.

"Get outta there!" said Brian over the subspace intercom. "Get away from that jamming device!"

Aaxtchu worked the controls desperately, trying to compensate not only for the reversed functions of the controls, but the continuing hail of sparks emitting from his instrument panel. He almost hit the Cardwick water tower. Then he did a loop-the-loop and nearly crashed into the town's only carwash. Finally, Aaxtchu somehow managed to veer away from the blue-lipped Earthling with her deadly device.

But Aaxtchu was now flying out of control, too fast and way too low, and he was forced to crash-land —again. He was dazed, confused, and now livid with annoyance. And to make matters worse, when Aaxtchu managed to see out of the cockpit, he found that he'd crashed once again into the backyard of an Earthling home.

"Buckaroo banzai!" was all he could say.

CHAPTER 12

AT HANNAH'S HOUSE, Mia and Hannah parked their bikes and went into the kitchen. Mia sat in a chair at the kitchen table while Hannah rummaged in the kitchen cupboards and cabinets for a frying pan, mixing spoon, and other things to make her bizarre snack. When she'd found the frying pan, she placed it on the burner and tossed in a pat of butter.

Hannah had gotten the radio to work, but there was no mention of the vandalism of the park, so they were listening to a classical music station. Mia wanted to listen to pop music, but Hannah said, "Bach and Vivaldi music help me think."

"Your thinking processes seem to need a lot of help," said Mia.

"You have no idea," said Hannah as she searched a drawer for a can opener.

Hannah got the can of meat open and tipped the contents into the frying pan. The odor of mystery meat filled the kitchen. Mia scrunched up her nose.

"You know, Mia," Hannah said as she stirred in the pineapple and ketchup. "I've been thinking about something that Mrs. Kramer said."

"What's that?" Mia asked, holding her nose.

"She said that Mr. Norris had bought a *whole case* of those candybars to give away to trick-or-treaters on Halloween."

"Yeah," said Mia. "That was awfully nice of him. But what's that got to do with Mike Johnson or the park graffiti?"

"Well, we went trick-or-treating together, and we went fairly early in the evening, right?"

"Right," answered Mia.

The mystery meat, pineapple, and ketchup mixture was bubbling and boiling now. The aroma was not a pleasant one. Hannah stirred it idly, thinking and musing.

Hannah asked, "I don't remember getting a jumbo-sized Ga-Ga Gooey Bar at Mr. Norris's house. Do you?"

Mia, still squeezing her nose shut against the outlandish food smells, narrowed her eyes and looked at the ceiling. "No. I believe Mr. Norris had turned off his porch light and had set out a bowl of saltwater taffy with a note that read, *Please take as many as you want. Please.*"

"Hey, that's right!" cried Hannah, turning her attention away from the frying pan. "And as everyone knows, the only people who give out salt-water taffy on Halloween are those who have run out of *real* candy."

"That's true," said Mia.

Hannah opened her purse and dug out the pencil and notebook. She tossed them in Mia's direction and said, "Hurry and write that down in the evidence notebook."

Mia picked up the pencil, opened the notebook, and began to write.

The mystery meat, ketchup, and pineapple sizzled on the oven. Hannah didn't notice, but it was now producing an oily gray smoke.

"Something about this seems fishy," said Hannah. "I think the next person we interview should be Mr. Norris. He's not a suspect, but he may have some interesting information for us. He's a 'person of inter-est'. Write that down."

Mia was struggling to write and hold her nose at the same time. "Hey, Hannah," she said, "are you done cooking now?" she asked, pointing to the frying pan, which was now billowing startling amounts of hot, black smoke. Just then, the smoke alarm in Hannah's kitchen was triggered, and a high, electronic wailing sound split the air.

"On second thought," screamed Hannah over the alarm noise. "I think this new dish of mine is not to my liking." Hannah opened a kitchen window and set the smoking pan on the window sill. Soon the alarm stopped its high-pitched alarm sound.

"Well, Mia, let's saddle up and head over to Mr. Norris's house," said Hannah as she turned off the stove.

The smoke alarm was silent now, but out in the backyard, Hannah's dog, Orson, was barking like mad.

"What's wrong with Orson?" Mia asked.

"Who knows," said Hannah with a wave of her hand. She didn't even bother to glance into the backyard. "He's probably annoyed by the smoke alarm. Or maybe he spotted a squirrel."

CHAPTER 13

Aaxtchu somehow managed to scramble out of the bottom hatch of his upside-down landing craft. Now he sat down on the grass and tried to clear his head.

"Aaxtchu?" Brian's voice crackled in the subspace intercom. "Aaxtchu, come in. Are you all right?"

Aaxtchu activated his subspace intercom and said, "Once again—no! I am not *all right*. I have been thwarted again by the blue-lipped Earthling!"

"That's a bummer," said Brian. "Are you injured? How's the landing craft?"

Aaxtchu sighed and stood. Then he deactivated the invisibility technology and walked around the ship, looking for damage.

"The landing craft seems undamaged," said

Aaxtchu, "but the electronic feedback from that Earthling's anti-spacecraft device has overheated the instruments. I must allow it to cool before I can fly again."

"Aaxtchu," said Brian. "I don't want to alarm you, but I should tell you that my sensors show that there are two smallish Earthlings in the nearby building. I think they're the same Earthlings that forced you to crash-land! Be careful!"

Aaxtchu's alien blood went cold. It was supposed to be cold, of course, but it got colder than normal. As cold as one of those slushy drinks you can get at Kramer's store. Aaxtchu sprang into action. First he activated the cloaking technology of the landing craft so that the small ship was invisible again. Then he hid behind a tree. It was a tall and narrow tree, but so was Aaxtchu, so it worked out well.

But it was too late.

An ear-piercing alarm suddenly emitted from the house.

"The hostile Earthlings have spotted me!" hissed Aaxtchu into the subspace intercom. "They've sounded an alarm! Surely their planetary defense troops will soon arrive to take me prisoner!"

"Run! Hide!" Brian shouted.

But in another moment, Aaxtchu was enveloped in a thick, oily smoke that billowed from a back window of the Earthling house. A defensive smoke screen! Not only did it fill the backyard with a dense black fog, but Aaxtchu's planetary suit sensors notified him that the smoke was highly toxic.

"Now they're trying to poison me with a toxic smoke screen!"

"You've got to evacuate the area, Aaxy!" Brian shouted into the subspace intercom. "You gotta get outta there!"

Aaxtchu tried, but he found himself in an area that was surrounded by a tall fence, and if that wasn't bad enough, Aaxtchu suddenly encountered a small but very frightening Earthling organism. It had four legs, a waggy tail, and a coating of thick fur. It was also equipped with a mouth full of small but very sharp-looking teeth. Aaxtchu realized it was the same creature he had encountered while looking for the landing craft's key. It growled and yapped and lunged aggressively at Aaxtchu. He recoiled and screamed into his subspace intercom.

"And now a blood-thirsty beast is attacking me!" he cried. "Brian! Help me or I am done for!"

"Aaxy!" said Brian. "My sensors show that the hostile Earthlings are leaving the area. If you can

93

fend off the deadly Earthling beast, you might survive! From what I've learned on the Earthling Internet, that kind of Earth beast has a fascination for the branches of Earth trees."

"A fascination for *what?*" screamed Aaxtchu. As he was running around the tree and the rest of the yard, the vicious guard monster nipped at the heels of his planetary suit. "What are you talking about?"

"The woody debris that falls off those large trees of Earth," Brian explained frantically through the subspace intercom. "See if you can find a stick or branch. Offer it to the Earth demon, and then throw it far away! It's your only chance, Aaxy!"

Aaxtchu looked around and spotted the kind of thing Brian described. It was a small piece of the tree he'd been hiding behind. As he ran from the Earth beast, he scooped it up in his skinny fingers. Then, mustering all his courage, he turned to the furry and vicious monster and held out the stick.

The dog instantly stopped its yapping and chasing. In fact, it sat in the grass and eyed the "stick" with great anticipation.

"I have offered the stick to the monster, and he has ceased attacking," whispered Aaxtchu into his subspace intercom. "What—do I do—next?"

Brian's voice came over the subspace intercom. "Okay. You have to listen to me very carefully."

Aaxtchu swallowed hard and whispered, "I am ready. Continue."

"Throw—the—stick," breathed Brian.

Aaxtchu blinked. Purple sweat was dripping down his face. "Throw it where?"

"Anywhere. Just throw it as far as you can."

Aaxtchu did as Brian instructed. He tossed the stick to the other side of the yard.

And it worked. The blood-thirsty defense creature ran off in the direction Aaxtchu had thrown the stick!

"Brian! I am saved!" said Aaxtchu with great relief. "The trick worked! The vicious monster has gone away!"

But then the monster returned. It held the stick in its deadly, slavering jaws.

"Oh, no!" cried Aaxtchu. "The monster returns! Now what?"

"Is he attacking?" asked Brian.

"No," said Aaxtchu with wonder in his voice. "He is peaceful now."

"Okay," said Brian quietly. "Carefully take the stick from the beast and throw it again."

Aaxtchu did so. The monster retrieved the stick again and brought it back to Aaxtchu.

"I believe the defense monster wishes me to repeat the stick-throwing," said Aaxtchu.

"Yeah," said Brian. "My research of the Earthling Internet tells me this is a ritual or game called, 'fetch'."

"How long must I participate in *fetch*?" said Aaxtchu, an undertone of panic entering his voice.

"Let me check," said Brian.

There was a pause while Brian checked the Earthling Internet. The Earthling beast sat very quietly, waiting for Aaxtchu to throw the stick again.

Then Brian's voice crackled over the subspace intercom again. "I have bad news, Aaxy."

"What is it?" moaned Aaxtchu.

"The 'fetch' game has no time limits," replied Brian. "It says here the game can go on indefinitely. You may be trapped for quite some time."

CHAPTER 14

Mr. Norris lived just around the block from Hannah. Frequently, she'd be out riding her bike when Mr. Norris was working in his garden, and she often stopped to chat with him. Mr. Norris lived by himself, and his children and grandchildren all lived far away, so he appreciated Hannah's visits.

However, she asked the strangest questions, like, "Would you rather step on chewed gum or have your glasses fog up?" or "How much could someone pay you to eat a spider?"

Still, Mr. Norris found Hannah quite funny and likeable, and he enjoyed speaking with her, so when Hannah and Mia showed up at his house, he welcomed them inside for cookies and milk.

Hannah dunked her cookie in the milk and took a bite.

"Mmm," she said, nodding her head. "Peanut butter and chocolate chips. This will definitely assist my thought processes."

"I think it's helping mine, too," said Mia. "Thank you, Mr. Norris."

"Do you happen to have any spicy mustard to go with these cookies?" asked Hannah.

Mr. Norris wrinkled his nose and said, "I'm not sure."

Hannah took a big swig of milk and wiped away the resulting milk moustache with her sleeve. "Don't worry about it. Strangely, these cookies are actually pretty good *without* mustard. Thanks a lot, Mr. Norris."

"Sure thing," said Mr. Norris. "It's nice to have some company."

Hannah finished her cookie and then swallowed the rest of her milk in one big gulp.

"Well, sir," she said. "I'm sorry to inform you that this is not a social call. We can arrange something more light-hearted at a future date, but Mia and I have some important questions about your Halloween candy-distribution policy."

Mr. Norris chuckled. "Oh, is that so? Well, please ask any questions you need to."

Hannah unzipped her purse and took out her

99

tube of blue lipstick and one of the compact mirrors. Mr. Norris smiled, sat back in his chair, crossed his legs, and waited for Hannah to freshen up her trademark lipstick.

"First," said Hannah applying the blue make-up, "let me ask you—did you have a pleasant Halloween?"

"I had a wonderful Halloween," said Mr. Norris. "In fact, it was—"

Hannah held up a finger. "Hold on a sec," she said. She rubbed her lips together then returned the lipstick and mirror to her purse. Next, she pulled out the pencil and evidence notepad and passed them to Mia. "More notes, please," she said. Then Hannah turned back to Mr. Norris, "So you said you had a very good Halloween?"

"Why is she taking notes?" Mr. Norris asked.

"Don't worry," said Hannah. "It's just so I can review your answers later and possibly submit them to the police as evidence."

"Oh, I see," said Mr. Norris, surprised. "So this really is not a social call."

"No, I wish I could say it was, but as I mentioned, we can arrange something more casual later."

"I must say, Hannah," said Mr. Norris. "You

always have the most fascinating things to talk about, and you go about conversation in the most interesting way."

"I try my best," Hannah replied. "And I appreciate your willingness to cooperate. So, did you get a lot of trick-or-treaters?"

"More than I was expecting. Sadly, I ran out of candy quite early," said Mr. Norris.

"What time would you say that was?" Hannah asked.

"Oh, I don't know. Maybe 6:00 or 6:30?"

Hannah turned to Mia. "That is *really* early. It's not even dark by then." She looked back at Mr. Norris and said, "Can you estimate how many kids came by before you ran out?"

"I can guess pretty accurately," said Mr. Norris, "because I bought a case of fifty jumbo-sized Ga-Ga Gooey Bars."

"I love Ga-Ga Gooey Bars," Mia said.

"So do I," said Hannah.

"So does everyone," said Mr. Norris, "which is why I saved five of them for myself. Sadly, they're all gone now, or I'd offer a couple to you girls. But I just couldn't resist eating them. Pretty sad, considering that Halloween wasn't that long ago."

"I don't know how anyone can resist eating Ga-

Ga Gooey Bars," said Hannah. "If I had five of them, I'd have eaten them all by now, too."

"Did you stop by my place on Halloween?" asked Mr. Norris. "I don't recall. Did you two get the Ga-Ga Gooeys?"

Hannah and Mia shook their heads.

"We came by quite early in the evening, but we were too late, apparently," said Mia. "You were already out."

"Oh, so you got the saltwater taffy I set on the porch? I'm awfully sorry about that."

"That's okay," said Hannah.

"Well, at least tell me about your Halloween costumes," said Mr. Norris.

"I was costumed as Madame Marie Curie, the ill-fated 19th-century French-Polish physicist who pioneered the research of radioactive and fissile materials" said Hannah.

"Oooh," said Mr. Norris. "That's very impressive. And what about you, Mia?"

"Bunny rabbit. Just a regular one. From *this* century."

"I'm very sorry I missed you. Your costumes sound very interesting and original, unlike the trick-or-treaters who came here on Halloween. They all had very similar costumes. There wasn't very much variety."

Hannah tilted her head and leaned in. "Could you please explain what you mean by that?"

"Well, in previous years, you kids have shown a lot of originality when it comes to costumes. But I've never seen so many kids wearing so many similar costumes and masks as this year. It seemed like every time I answered the door, I saw the same few costumes over and over."

Hannah's eyes were wide, and she sat on the edge of her seat now. "What costumes did you see?" She tapped on the notebook Mia was holding to signal her to write them down.

"Uh, let's see. There was a magician, vampire, ghost, and pirate. Oh, and the one I really remember was that little bug character who wears a tuxedo."

"A bug in a tuxedo?" Hannah asked. "Why would someone dress up like a bug in a tuxedo?"

"I think he's talking about Mr. Max," said Mia. "It's a popular character from the video game *Superbugs of the Ultraverse*. Is that right, Mr. Norris?"

"Yes, Mr. Max," said Mr. Norris. "The bug with the tuxedo and one long antenna. I don't know anything about Mr. Max or the video game, but I've seen my grandkids playing it."

103

"Don't you mean *two* antennae?" Mia asked. "Mr. Max has two antennae, like all bugs."

"Hmm. No, I'm quite sure. All the Mr. Max costumes had just *one* antenna," said Mr. Norris.

Hannah narrowed her eyes and asked, "Mr. Norris, is there any possibility, any possibility at all, that you had the *same* handful of kids coming to your house over and over again?"

Mr. Norris tilted his head. "No, I don't think so. I would have noticed if the same kids with the same costumes kept coming back, and I'd have told them to skeedaddle. I saw the same costumes, but I saw tall Mr. Maxes and short Mr. Maxes. I saw a pirate with blue sneakers and another with white sneakers. I saw one vampire with a cape, but others with no cape. It was the costumes that were the same, not the kids, although I did notice most of them were quite tall. They were probably a little too old to be trick-or-treating."

"But you're certain that all the Mr. Max costumes had just *one* antenna?" asked Hannah.

"Yeah, positive," answered Mr. Norris. "Why do you ask?"

"Oh, it's probably nothing," said Hannah. "Can we help you clean up these cookies and milk?"

"No, no," said Mr. Norris. "I'll take care of

them."

Mr. Norris walked the girls to the door and looked outside. "What a nice day it is," he said.

"Yeah," said Hannah. "Unseasonably warm. Your grass and flowerbeds seem kinda dried up."

"You're right," replied Mr. Norris, placing his hands on his hips. "Maybe I ought to start up the sprinklers."

"I was just going to suggest that," said Hannah. "Well, we must be going." Hannah put on her sunglasses and said, "Come, Mia. To the bikes!"

"You girls have a nice day," said Mr. Norris. "And come back when you've solved whatever mystery you're working on!"

"We will," said Hannah. "Thank you again for the cookies!"

After Mia and Hannah were back on the road, Hannah asked, "Well, what do you think?"

"Something strange is definitely going on," said Mia. "I play *Superbugs of the Ultraverse*, and Mr. Max always has two antennae. It doesn't make sense. And I still don't understand how this has anything to do with the case of the spray paint in the park. I don't get it!"

"Don't worry, Mia," said Hannah with a clever smile on her face. "You will soon."

CHAPTER 15

AGAINST WHAT SEEMED like impossible odds, Aaxtchu had at last reached the wide-open farm field where he'd planned to configure and install the device that would rid the atmosphere of Earth of its hideous and stinky oxygen, which in turn would clear the way for the intergalactic construction crews to commence building their vacation homes. Aaxtchu had crashed into a garden shed. He'd crash-landed and lost his keys not once but twice (each). And he'd had to play a terrifying game of "fetch" with a slavering and vicious Earth attack monster for what seemed like twenty chronoplops (it was actually just one hour). He'd been poisoned with smoke and pursued and frightened out of his gigantic mind, but now he was finally ready to complete his mission.

Aaxtchu was exhausted, annoyed, and flabbergasted. (Incidentally, Aaxtchu's word for "exhausted" was "plifferblated," and his word for "annoyed" was "galonked," but Aaxtchu and Brian's word for "flabbergasted" was in fact "flabbergasted"—just one of those strange linguistic coincidences.)

And so Aaxtchu released a great sigh and then reminded himself that all the trouble and crashing and dangerous alien encounters would be well worth it once he and his friends and family were able to take a nice long vacation on Earth. He couldn't help picturing himself sipping a tall hot glass of Krolian lemonade while the children played Hyperborean hide-and-seek (a game similar to Earthling hide-and-seek in most ways, but with much more dire consequences).

It was this thought alone that gave Aaxtchu the willpower to land his landing craft and haul out the de-oxygenator.

The machine itself was quite large, taller even than Aaxtchu. It was shaped like a cone, and had one big tube protruding from it, which is where it gathered in all the oxygen. There were lots of lights and buttons on the machine, but its actual operation was quite simple. Once it was in place, all Aaxtchu had to do was flip a switch, and the machine would start removing all the oxygen from Earth.

But unbeknownst to Aaxtchu, when Mr. Norris's sprinklers activated, Mrs. Mable Moser across the street had seen them, and she had decided that she probably ought to turn on her sprinklers, too, which she did. And as Mr. Bradley Budds was driving home from work, he saw Mrs. Moser's sprinklers sprinkling, which led him to decide that he ought to water his grass, as well. Mr. Wyatt Wheatley down the street couldn't help but see the sprinklers of Mrs. Moser and Mr. Budds, so he turned his sprinklers on in his farm field, too—the same field where Aaxtchu was configuring the de-oxygenator.

Now the thing about water is that its chemical properties are H_2O (or, more accurately "dihydrogen monoxide" meaning it has two hydrogen atoms and one oxygen atom). Aaxtchu's people loved hydrogen. They would take deep breaths of hydrogen and always found it extraordinarily refreshing. But to Aaxtchu's people, oxygen was poison.

And so when the sprinklers turned on and started spraying Aaxtchu and his machine and ship with small particles of hydrogen and oxygen, bad things started happening. The water began to dissolve Aaxtchu's protective planetary suit, and the circuitry of the de-oxygenator began to spark and smoke.

Aaxtchu immediately called Brian on the subspace intercom to find out what to do next, but both Brian and Aaxtchu were beginning to think that planet Earth was cursed.

CHAPTER 16

MIA AND HANNAH stood in front of the Cardwick City Library.

"It's getting kinda late," said Mia. "I'm going to have to head home for dinner soon."

"Not to worry, Mia dear," replied Hannah. "We are nearly at the end of our quest."

"You keep saying that," said Mia, "but I don't understand how it all fits together. Why are we here at the library?"

"I shall explain it, Mia. But first—" Hannah unzipped her purse and grabbed her bubble pipe. She also removed the bag with the Ga-Ga Gooey Bar wrapper that they'd found at the beginning of the investigation. Hannah blew a cloud of medium-sized but very thoughtful bubbles before continuing.

"Let me ask you this, Mia. If we had arrived at Mr. Norris's house on Halloween early enough to receive his very generous treat of a jumbo-sized Ga-Ga Gooey Bar, what would you do with it?"

"I'd eat it," replied Mia flatly.

"I see. You wouldn't save the candybar?" asked Hannah.

"No, I'd eat it."

"You wouldn't put it in the fridge and save it for some special occasion?"

"No."

"Wouldn't give it to your little sister?"

"No."

"Sell it to a classmate for a handsome profit?"

"No!"

"Feed it to the nanny goat up the road?"

"*No!*"

"Precisely!" exclaimed Hannah. "Neither would I! I'd have ripped the wrapper off right there on Mr. Norris's porch and chowed it down."

"Yeah, me too," said Mia. "So what?"

"So, let's say you received two or three Ga-Ga Gooey Bars on Halloween. Do you suppose you'd have any left now?"

"No way. I'd have eaten them already."

"Even if they were jumbo bars?"

"*Especially* if they were jumbo!"

"Yes, exactly. Me, too. Even Mr. Norris kept five for himself, and he's already eaten them. He couldn't resist."

"All right," said Mia. "What's it all mean?"

"Answer me this, Mia," Hannah continued. "Do you or anyone else in Cardwick have a way to get any additional Ga-Ga Gooey Bars?"

"No, I don't think so—Mrs. Kramer told us nationwide supplies were very limited, and she hadn't had any in stock since before Halloween."

"That's right!" shouted Hannah.

She held up the paint-stained Ga-Ga Gooey Bar wrapper from the park and waved it under Mia's nose enticingly. Mia caught a whiff of the chocolatey aroma and breathed in deeply.

"Mmm," she said.

"So," Hannah went on. "The question we must answer is this: how did anyone in Cardwick still have a jumbo-sized Ga-Ga Gooey Bar so long after Halloween, in the park, while the vandalism was going on?"

Mia nodded and thought about this. She couldn't think of the answer, so she thought about it some more. And then it came to her. Her eyes flew open wide. "The person who dropped this wrapper on the night of the vandalism must have had *lots* of Ga-Ga Gooey Bars!"

"Correct, my dear Mia!"

But then Mia frowned. "I still don't understand how it fits together, though."

"It's elementary, Mia! You're so close!" Hannah handed Mia the evidence notebook. "With all we now know, knowing all we've discovered, how would someone in Cardwick get their hands on a big supply of these precious, jumbo-sized candy delights?"

Mia flipped through the notebook and studied each set of notes page by page. Hannah stood tapping her foot on the concrete sidewalk, her arms folded and her big sunglasses aimed at the lowering sun. She didn't have to pace now—she'd solved the mystery.

"To have enough Ga-Ga Gooey bars to last this long after Halloween," Mia said, thinking out loud, "there was only one source—Mr. Norris!"

"Right!" cried Hannah.

"So, Mr. Norris is the culprit?"

"No," said Hannah. "Don't be silly."

Mia's mouth dropped open. She'd realized something. "One of Mr. Norris's trick-or-treaters is the vandal!"

"Now you've got it!" Hannah said, patting Mia on the shoulder.

"Wow! I got it!" cried Mia. "We solved the mystery!"

Hannah shook her head, held up one finger, and said, "Not. Quite."

"Oh. Because how would the trick-or-treaters get more than one of the candybars? And how could we find out who the trick-or-treaters were if they were all wearing masks and costumes?" said Mia.

"I had the same question, Mia. But then *you* caught the final clue, and it all fell into place. You pointed out the discrepancy of Mr. Max's single antenna."

"Oh, yeeeah," said Mia, placing a finger on her chin. "That's a really weird clue—why *did* all the Mr. Max masks have only one antenna when Mr. Max has two?"

Hannah drew close to Mia and blew one large and very dramatic bubble from the pipe. Then, in a low and equally dramatic voice she said, "Because, Mia. There weren't mistable Master Mask Maxes—whoa. That's really quite hard to say. I ruined my reveal. Pretend you didn't hear that and let me do it again. Give me a minute."

Mia nodded, leaned on her bike, and waited for Hannah to compose herself.

Hannah turned around, arranged her hair, straightened her sunglasses, and then faced Mia once more. Hannah then blew a new stream of extremely wise bubbles, leaned in close to Mia, and said, "Because! There were *not* multiple Mr. Max masks! There was only *one* Mr. Max mask, but on Halloween night, it was worn on multiple faces!"

An expression of shock and dismay crossed Mia's face. "Nooo," she said in a breathy voice. "You can't mean it. Double-dipping trick-or-treaters?"

"It's sad but true," said Hannah nodding. "Double-dipping, triple-dipping, and perhaps even octuple-dipping trick-or-treaters!"

Mia closed her eyes and slowly shook her head. "I can't believe it. Multi-dipping is the most nefarious trick in all of trick-or-treating!"

Hannah nodded and said, "Exactly."

Then Hannah bit down on her bubble pipe and blew hard. With that, the last of the soapy bubble mixture inside became an enormous flock of plump, wobbly bubbles, which floated upwards and caught the breeze, drifting off in the direction of the farm

115

fields on the west side of town. Mia and Hannah watched them go.

"Now," continued Hannah, "do you understand why we are here at the library?"

Mia narrowed her eyes and nodded. "Let's go close this case!"

CHAPTER 17

Oᴜᴛ ɪɴ ᴛʜᴇ middle of Mr. Wyatt Wheatley's alfalfa field, Aaxtchu tugged and pulled and strained to get the all-important de-oxygenator back onto the landing craft so that it would not be damaged by the deluge of oxygen-rich sprinkler water. Aaxtchu's task was made more difficult because the landing craft was currently invisible, and in case you don't know, it's always just a little more complicated to load machinery into a space-craft you can't see. And as if that weren't bad enough, Mr. Wheatley's field was getting progres-sively muddier with every passing chronoblip. And so Aaxtchu slipped and slid in the mucky mud. His spacesuit was splattered with dark, muddy earth, and it was difficult to keep hold of the de-oxygenator because it was now so wet.

"What's going on down there?" said Brian to Aaxtchu over the subspace intercom.

"I am experiencing a seemingly endless procession of difficulties," replied Aaxtchu, grunting and growling as he heaved the de-oxygenator into the cloaked landing craft. "I have become drenched in deadly H_2O! And the de-oxygenator, too, is covered in H_2O. I am in a perilous situation!"

"Wow," said Brian. "This really just is not your chronoturn, is it?"

"No!" shouted Aaxtchu into the subspace intercom. "In fact, this is one of the worst chronoturns I can recall!"

"My sensors aren't showing any weather patterns that might result in H_2O dispersal," said Brian. "How did you get drenched and muddy?"

"There appears to be some kind of widespread automatic defensive weapon system that sprays poison!" Aaxtchu complained loudly. "The Earthlings' sensors have evidently detected my presence once again, and I wouldn't be surprised if that little conniving, blue-lipped Earthling had something to do with it!"

"Well," said Brian, "I'm sorry you're having such a bad chronoturn, but do you think you can give me an estimate on when you'll be finished down there?

119

I'd like to knock off for the day and maybe cook up some Betazoid burgers. I think we have a few bottles of Leola root beer, too. How much longer is this gonna take you?"

Aaxtchu shouted something at Brian through the subspace intercom, an insult that translates roughly into English like this: "I hope you get sucked into a massive black hole, and then the black hole increases in mass until it is a quasar!" Then he cut off the intercom and returned to his task.

Of course, as soon as Aaxtchu had gotten the de-oxygenator into the invisible landing craft, the automated H_2O defensive sprayers stopped spraying. That was just the kind of chronoturn Aaxy was having. And in only a few chronoblips more, the warm sun began to dry the ground. Aaxtchu knew he had to drag the thing back out.

Exhausted, Aaxtchu slumped against the de-oxygenator. This whole mission had been so much more difficult than he had ever imagined it might be, and he was beginning to think that he and Brian had chosen the wrong planet for their vacation retreat. Perhaps there was a different planet that already had the right atmosphere and beautiful scenery, but did not have meddlesome little juveniles like the blue-lipped Earthling. Why hadn't they investigated

Saturn? It was an attractive world, with its many moons and beautiful rings of cosmic dust. Or there was Jupiter, where there were titanic cliffs of lava and ice, tipped with hydrogen flaming at the tops. And what about Planet 10? He'd *always* wanted to journey to the 8th Dimension to see Planet 10. Aaxtchu was experiencing major regrets about ever coming to Earth.

But the mission could still be saved, Aaxtchu told himself. He was so close now—all he had to do was drag the de-oxygenator back out into the farm field, configure it, activate it, and wait a mere ten chronoplops.

"You can do this, Aaxy!" he growled to himself. "You can do it!"

And so he did it. With renewed strength, Aaxtchu practically hoisted the de-oxygenator over his head, set it in the middle of Mr. Wheatley's field, and started pressing buttons and flipping switches and turning dials. A flurry of red, green, and blue lights flashed. There was a whirring sound that turned into a steady whizzing sound that became a low pulsing drone.

It was working!

"At last!" cried Aaxtchu.

Aaxtchu's sensors showed that the level of

121

dreadful oxygen in the immediate area was already dropping. For the first time all day, Aaxtchu smiled. (Oddly, Aaxtchu's smile looked exactly like the expression known as a "frown" on Earth.)

The de-oxygenator had the ability to take in and eliminate tremendous amounts of oxygen. But, obviously, the de-oxygenator couldn't just make the oxygen vanish. That would be against the laws of physics, and if there was one thing Aaxtchu did, it was obey the law. No, the oxygen had to be converted into something else, and in this case, Aaxtchu had set the machine to convert the oxygen to small chunks of a delicious delicacy called "Chunklybunkly."

What Aaxtchu had no way of knowing was that Chunklybunkly looked and tasted exactly like Ga-Ga Gooey Bars (but contained in a plain wrapper). Aaxtchu removed one of the chunks from the output tray and put it in his pocket for later.

"Slithy toves, gyre gimble!" shouted Aaxtchu, which is to say, "Goodbye oxygen, hello vacation!"

And with that, Aaxtchu sat down on the invisible bumper of the landing craft to let the de-oxygenator work its magic. As he sat there, he saw something sparkling in the sky. It was a collection of transparent spheres that wobbled and wafted on the wind. They were very pretty to look at, and they were floating closer, but Aaxtchu's space-traveler instincts told him that this was not a good thing, and tiny beads of purple sweat sprang up on his forehead.

The first of the glimmering little spheres floated right over to Aaxtchu, and so he held up one long finger to touch it.

And it popped!

Only a small droplet of soapy liquid was left, which fell to the ground.

Now an entire flock of the little soapy spheres were floating down on the breeze, and to Aaxtchu's alarm, the de-oxygenator was pulling them in through its intake valve! Aaxtchu frowned (which, of course, looked like an Earthling smile).

"Ropely wopely mopely," he said, which when translated means something like: "Hoo boy. This can't be good."

It would take several chronoblips to turn off the de-oxygenator, and so Aaxtchu ran in a tight circle around the de-oxygenator, trying to shoo the swarming soapy spheres away, but the machine was too efficient, and it slurped in every single one of them.

Now, instead of the low pulsing sound the

machine was supposed to make, the de-oxygenator made a wild hissing and zapping sound. The soapy substance of the spheres were shorting out the circuitry, contaminating the sensors, and frying the conversion cells. In less than a single chronoblip, the de-oxygenator was clanging and shrieking and belching out great quantities of blue and yellow fog.

Aaxtchu took a cautious step back, then another. "Ropely wopely mopely *dopely!*" he cried, which when translated means, "This is going to be super terrible!"

Aaxtchu knew this was probably his last try to make Earth into a vacation planet for his people, and he barely had time to leap behind the landing craft before the de-oxygenator exploded. Inside the crater created by the explosion, nothing remained but a few shards of obliterated circuitry and thousands of fragments of Chunklybunkly.

CHAPTER 18

HANNAH AND MIA parked their bikes in the bike rack outside the Cardwick City Library and climbed the steps to the front doors. They passed through the doors and into the library, then marched up to the librarian's desk.

"Hello, girls," said the librarian, Ms. Persimmon. "Good to see you at the library today."

"Hi, Ms. Persimmon," said Hannah. "This is Mia and I'm Hannah. We both have interesting name spellings, but we're too short on time to explain. As you might know, I am Cardwick's foremost junior private sleuth and detective."

"I feel like both of those words mean the same thing," said Ms. Persimmon, "but please do go on."

Hannah produced her wallet and flipped it open

to reveal some kind of official identification card, which she flashed at Ms. Persimmon like a badge.

(It was a library card.)

Ms. Persimmon looked closely at the card and said, "Oh, how fun. Your first name is spelled the same way forwards and backwards. A palindrome!"

Hannah nodded. "Yes, ma'am."

"And, Mia, I presume your name is spelled M-I-A, meaning that when it's reversed, it spells the word *aim*."

Mia nodded. "That's correct, ma'am."

"Well, now," said Ms. Persimmon, "with that settled, I am at your service. What can I do to help?"

"Thank you for your cooperation," said Hannah, putting away her wallet. "We're gonna need to see the archival copies of the newspaper from November first, the day after Halloween."

"Of course," said Ms. Persimmon. She was quite possibly the most polite person Hannah had ever met. "Step right this way."

Ms. Persimmon led the girls to a room where recent copies of the town's only newspaper, the *Cardwick Communicator*, were kept.

"Please let me know if you need any further assistance, ladies," said Ms. Persimmon. "I must caution you, however, that the library will be closing in just fifteen minutes."

"Then we must get to work," said Hannah.

"Thank you, Ms. Persimmon," said Mia.

Ms. Persimmon inclined her head politely and left the room.

Turning to Mia, Hannah said, "Every year on the day after Halloween, the *Communicator* always features photos of people in Halloween costumes from all over town."

"So, we just need to see if we can spot the costumes that Mr. Norris mentioned," said Mia.

"Right. But we don't have much time!"

The girls pored over the newspaper. There were dozens of photos from various Halloween parades and parties and trick-or-treating.

"Look!" said Mia, pointing. "There's Thad Thacker in the vampire costume and Matt Madison in the pirate costume! Just like Mr. Norris said!"

"Good eye, Mia," said Hannah. "Oh, and look here! It's Steven Stephens in a magician's costume!"

"Here!" cried Mia. "It's Thad Thacker who's wearing the magician hat and cape, and Matt Madison dressed as the vampire! They really were trading costumes!"

"All we need to do now is find Mr. Max!" said

Mia. "But there are so many kids wearing Mixer Mask Maxes. Whoa, you're right—that *is* hard to say. There are so many kids wearing *Mr. Max masks!*"

"Right, but as you noted, the Mr. Max costume Mr. Norris saw had only *one* antenna. The other was probably broken off during some form of Halloween merriment. Look for the mask with only one antenna."

The two girls continued, intensely scanning the pictures in the paper. Just then, there was a series of soft, musical tones on a loudspeaker, and then they heard Ms. Persimmon's polite and delightful voice.

"Attention Cardwick City Library patrons. The library shall close in five minutes. Please conclude your business and make your way to the front desk or the nearest exit. Thank you."

"It's too much pressure!" cried Hannah, rubbing her face with her hand. "What if we can't find the photos? Mia, I'm freaking out!"

"Pull yourself together and keep looking, Hannah!" cried Mia.

The girls shuffled the papers, their eyes darting desperately from photo to photo.

"There!" said Mia at last and without a minute to spare. She was tapping a picture of a boy wearing a Mr. Max costume, the mask of which had only one antenna. And the mask was pushed up onto the boy's forehead, but his face was blurry.

"Drat! Drat! Drat! Who is it?" growled Hannah, squinting at the page. "I can't tell!"

Mia bent down until her nose was almost touching the paper. Then she held her hand out to Hannah and said, "Magnifying glass, please."

Hannah rummaged frantically in her purse and passed her magnifying glass to Mia, who placed the glass over the photo and squinted with almost superhuman effort.

"I know who it is!" cried Mia. "The one-antennaed Mr. Max is none other than Mrs. Kramer's stock-boy! It's Scott Scamperson!"

"We've got 'em!" shouted Hannah triumphantly.

"Ladies, if you please!" It was Ms. Persimmon, who had appeared suddenly but somehow still very politely at the door to the newspaper room. "We maintain a quiet, contemplative mood here in the library."

"Yes, ma'am," said Hannah with a quick curtsy. "Our apologies, of course."

"Well, now," Ms. Persimmon continued. "If you are, as you say, Cardwick's foremost junior private sleuth and detective, I presume you'll need photocopies of the research you've uncovered here today?"

"Oh, dear lady," said Hannah, with a second, deeper curtsy, "that would be more helpful than you could ever know."

Photocopies cost five cents apiece at the Cardwick City Library, but Ms. Persimmon waived this fee after Mia explained that they'd expended all of their pocket change on candy bars and Miss Mongo's Mystery Meat.

Only when they'd thoroughly expressed their heartfelt gratitude to the helpful and polite Ms. Persimmon did the girls leave the library. As they made their way to the bike rack, Mia thumbed through the photocopies.

"Hey," she said. "Hannah, do you notice something that all these boys have in common?"

"Of course," said Hannah, throwing a leg over her bike. "They have the costumes which were observed over and over again by Mr. Norris on Halloween."

"No, there's something else they all have in common. They're all on the White Timbers High School football team!"

CHAPTER 19

BACK ON THE navigation deck of the *Shiny Vessel that Travels so Smoothly from Star to Star*, Brian floated quickly over to Aaxtchu, or at least it looked like he was floating, because of his intergalactic robe. Aaxtchu had returned to the *Shiny Vessel that Travels so Smoothly from Star to Star* and changed out of his soaking wet, torn, and muddy planetary suit, and into his own more-comfy intergalactic robe. Nevertheless, Aaxtchu looked exhausted, angry, frustrated, and regretful all at the same time. It would be too difficult to describe what this looked like, but Aaxtchu looked as though he had aged five chronospans during his short time down on the Earth's surface. Brian was shocked when he saw his spaceship mate step onto the navigation deck.

"Aaxtchu! Bic zippo? Rimple dimple, Zarko foo

man choo!" said Brian, which in English would be translated into something like, "Aaxtchu! What in the galaxy happened to you? You look like you've been devoured by a Zarkonian rage-beast and spit out sideways!"

Aaxtchuu was staring at the giant monitor, where the blue, green, and white planet rotated slowly. From up there, on board the *Shiny Vessel that Travels so Smoothly from Star to Star*, planet Earth was a truly beautiful thing, like an intergalactic jewel. However, Aaxtchu now knew that it would be disastrous to de-oxygenate the planet and build vacation homes there. He pointed at the massive monitor.

"Ivewached see beems glit, erin thedarkoff tanhausergate," he said, his eyes wide and terrified. "Not this planet," he was saying. "We'll have to find another one."

"What?" said Brian. "But it's perfect. What happened to you down there?"

"Ull hod turden weir mudgaard gring nirurd rmoln irfenrirlukk Chunklybunkly," muttered Aaxtchu.

Translation: "I don't want to talk about it. I'm going to my quarters now to eat my Chunklybunkly and sleep for ten chronoplops."

CHAPTER 20

THE NEXT SATURDAY, Hannah and Mia sat on the front steps of Mia's house. Hannah had refilled her bubble pipe and was idly blowing swarms of bubbles that wobbled up on the evening breeze and gleamed in the beams of the setting sun.

Not much had happened in Cardwick since that day Mia and Hannah had rode their bikes at top speed from the library to the police station to present their sleuth work and evidence. It wasn't easy to get one of the officers to take them seriously, but as you may have noticed, Hannah is persistent. Brian and Aaxtchu would say she is "deedlish," which in English would mean something like, "really super difficult (perhaps even hazardous) to say 'no' to."

And so a nice police detective named Lieutenant Lifesaver had listened patiently as Hannah and Mia explained the fiendish plots of the White Timbers High School football players,

Thad Thacker, Matt Madison, Steven Stephens, and Scott Scamperson.

"They had trick-or-treated the city of Cardwick's entire supply of Ga-Ga Gooey Bars, you see," explained Hannah, showing photocopies of the newspaper photos. "They traded pieces of their costumes—masks, false vampire teeth, hats, capes, and so on—to make Mr. Norris *think* that they were different groups of trick-or-treaters. By changing into ten different costume combinations and returning to Mr. Norris's house approximately once per minute, they were able to pilfer all forty-five of the jumbo-sized Ga-Ga Gooey Bars before any other trick-or-treaters even got started!"

"That's fascinating, young lady," said Lieutenant Lifesaver, "but I don't see how this relates to the vandalism at the park."

"We did a stakeout at the park, sir," said Mia. "And we didn't spot any suspicious activity, but we did find this—"

Hannah produced the Ga-Ga Gooey Bar wrapper with blue and orange paint on it.

"A candy wrapper?" asked Lieutenant Lifesaver.

"Not just any candy wrapper," explained

135

Hannah. "This is the wrapper of a jumbo-sized Ga-Ga Gooey Bar, the candy bar which is very scarce right now due to aspects of supply and demand—you can talk to Mrs. Kramer and Mr. Norris about that."

"I see," said Lieutenant Lifesaver.

"Now," said Mia, "finding a candy wrapper in a park is no big deal, but this one is smeared with both blue and orange paint—the colors of spray paint that was not only in the vandalism at the park, but was also stolen from Mrs. Kramer's store. Whoever perpetrated the vandalism ate this candy bar, and in the process, transferred the incriminating spray paint to the wrapper, which they then discarded at the park."

"Go on," said Lieutenant Lifesaver.

Hannah said, "We know that the only people who were likely to have a jumbo-sized Ga-Ga Gooey Bar were the trick-or-treating multi-dippers, Thad Thacker, Matt Madison, and Steven Stephens, not to mention Scott Scamperson, who works at Mrs. Kramer's store! You see, Scott not only knew Mr. Norris had purchased an entire case of the candybars for the purposes of Halloween distribution, he also had access to the spray paint!"

Lieutenant Lifesaver raised an eyebrow. "Well, ladies, these are very interesting deductions and inferences, but I'm afraid it might not be enough to prove a case."

"We have additional facts," said Mia, opening Hannah's evidence notebook. "Did you notice that there were lots of misspelled words in the graffiti? In case you didn't know, Mike Johnson is a former spelling bee champion and would therefore never misspell, for instance, the word *lose* as *loose*. But if you check with our suspects, I'm almost sure you'll find at least one of them is flunking English."

Hannah picked up where Mia left off. "Mike Johnson can tell you that the letterman jacket found at the scene of the vandalism had been missing for weeks. Football players always wear their letterman jackets, especially when a big game is coming up. It's practically a uniform! But I bet if you ask around at Aspen High School, you won't find a single student or teacher who has seen Mike Johnson wearing his letterman jacket any time recently."

Mia handed the evidence notebook to Lieutenant Lifesaver, who thumbed through it, looking closely at the notes and diagrams. He nodded his head approvingly at times.

"As you can see," said Hannah, "the football players of White Timbers High sprayed the graffiti against their *own football team* in order to frame their rival quarterback, Mike Johnson, to increase their team's chances of winning the big championship game! With Mike Johnson kicked off the Aspen team, and the White Timbers players hungry for revenge for the poorly spelled graffiti, White Timbers High School was almost sure to win."

"Plus," added Lieutenant Lifesaver, tapping his finger on the notebook, "something like this would rally a lot of the community members to support and cheer for the White Timbers team instead of the Aspen team."

"Good point, sir!" said Hannah. "That's precisely what Mrs. Kramer told us."

Lieutenant Lifesaver smiled at Hannah and Mia. Then he said, "Wait here." He gathered up Hannah's evidence and notebook and discussed the matter with a few other police officers. Then he came back and said, "Listen, why don't you girls go on home."

"But our case!" said Hannah. "It's open and shut!"

"Our evidence!" cried Mia. "You can't ignore it!"

Hannah's lower lip quivered. Mia's eyes brimmed with trembling tears.

Lieutenant Lifesaver held up his hand. "No, no, no! I meant, why don't you girls just go on home—

and wait while I check out this new information and follow up on these leads! Sorry. I should have completed my entire thought before ending my sentence. You've obviously worked very hard, and the least I can do is snoop around a bit more."

However, Hannah didn't need any further assurances—she knew she'd cracked the case and that the culprits would be brought to justice.

And they were.

Thad Thacker, Matt Madison, Steve Stephens, and Scott Scamperson admitted that they'd cooked up the vandalism plot to win the big game. And they also confessed to a multi-dip trick-or-treating ring, which is not a crime but *is* a very serious breach of Halloween etiquette. Scott Scamperson was exposed as the ringleader. All four boys said they were sorry, and that they would never do anything like it again, but there were several consequences for them to deal with. Aside from the vandalism clean-up and repairs, Scott Scamperson lost his job at Kramer's for stealing the spray paint. And of course all four culprits were all grounded for various sentences, removed from the football team, and banned from trick-or-treating within the Cardwick city limits.

Scott Scamperson was additionally sent to an

after-school remedial spelling program to improve his marks in English.

With the star quarterback, Mike Johnson, restored to the Aspen High School football team, they played a great championship game. It was unfortunate, but White Timbers suffered a huge loss.

In the days that followed, Cardwick Mayor Jill Julep and Cardwick Police Chief Beatrice Boondock had phoned Hannah and Mia to thank them for their amateur detective work. Mike Johnson had also thanked the two sleuths—with a whole case of Ga-Ga Gooey Bars.

"Wow!" cried Hannah. "Where'd you find a whole case?"

"Mrs. Kramer finally got a new shipment," said Mike. "So I bought everything she had. It was the least I could do. Thank you so much for helping me."

But things had settled down after that.

There were a few remaining mysteries and conspiracies. For example, the entire town was at a loss to explain Mrs. Lemon's demolished garden shed.

"It was so well-built and solid," they said. "How could it have suffered so much damage without anyone noticing?"

Mr. Wheatley was claiming that aliens had

blown a huge crater in his alfalfa field—and that it was filled with curious circuitry and chunks of chocolate.

Hannah's own dog had for some strange reason developed a puzzling fondness for extremely long sessions of fetch.

However, after closing the epic Case of the Ga-Ga Gooey Graffiti, none of these lesser cases seemed very interesting to Hannah. And so on Saturday she sat on Mia's steps with her arms resting on her knees and her chin resting on her arms. The bubble pipe drooped from Hannah's blue lips, an obvious sign of her boredom and discouragement.

"Hey, Hannah," said Mia. "What's up? You seem a little down."

"Oh, I don't know," sighed Hannah. "Just the post-mystery-solving blues, I guess. It happened to Sherlock Holmes all the time."

"But you cracked the case and brought the real culprits to justice."

"*We* cracked the case," Hannah corrected. "I could never have done it without you."

"Yeah! And it feels great!"

"But we didn't save the world," mumbled Hannah. "Finding out who vandalized the park in Cardwick is hardly a world-saving thing. In fact, I don't even have that feeling anymore that the world *needs* saving. It went away." She sighed again. A trail of gloomy bubbles emerged from the pipe and floated slowly away.

Mia put a hand on Hannah's shoulder. "But we *did* save the world, Hannah! If you ask me, this is exactly how you save the world—you do good things wherever you happen to be."

"You really think so?" said Hannah, sitting up straighter.

"Yeah! If everyone just tries to help out in whatever way they can, wherever they're located, the world will always be getting better and better."

Hannah smiled. "Thanks, Mia. I think you're right!"

"Of course I'm right."

Then a strange expression began to appear on Hannah's face.

"Oh, boy," said Mia. "I know *that* look. You want to save the world again, don't you?"

"Yes. Grab your bike, Mia! We're off to Mrs. Lemon's garden shed!"

THANK you for joining me in the story of how Hannah and Mia saved the world. I hope you had as much fun reading the book as I had writing it.

If you have a few moments, it would mean the world to me if you would leave an honest review about the book on the retail site of your choice. Your help in spreading the word is greatly appreciated. Reviews from readers help make a huge difference in assisting new readers in finding books they'll enjoy.

May you keep reading and saving the world in your own way wherever you happen to be.

Love, A.M. Luzzader

P.S. If you'd like to know when my next book is out and also receive occasional updates on bonus offers, freebies, and special deals, please sign up for my newsletter at www.amluzzader.com.

A.M. Luzzader writes middle-grade books for children and science fiction books for adults. She is a self-described 'fraidy cat. Things she will run away from include (but are not limited to): mice, snakes, spiders, bits of string and litter that resemble spiders, most members of the insect kingdom, and (most especially) bats. Bats are the worst. But A.M. is first and primarily a mother to two energetic and intelligent sons, and this role inspires and informs her writing.

She was named Writer of the Year for 2019-2020 by the League of Utah Writers. A.M. invites readers to visit her website at www.amluzzader.com and her Facebook page www.facebook.com/authoramandaluzzader.

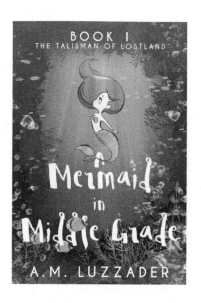

A Mermaid in Middle Grade: Book 1: The Talisman of Lostland

(Available now)

A young mermaid. A sea witch out for revenge. Can Brynn Finley become a sea guardian and help humans in danger when she just barely started the sixth grade?

Brynn Finley is the only mermaid in class who hasn't been able to learn mer-magic. Without it, she can't be a guardian of the sea with her parents and friends. On her quest for answers, Brynn encounters a loveable sea turtle, a pair of selkie sisters, and Phaedra, the great and terrible sea witch. Soon Brynn is over her head in trouble, and she must learn to ask for help if she's going to follow the merfolk oath to be a protector of the ocean and a guardian of the sea.

The Mermaid in Middle Grade series is a middle-grade fantasy adventure series and coming of age books appropriate for ages 8-12 and all who enjoy middle grade books.

Educational topics: Ocean and marine life, environmental conservation, honesty, friendship, mindfulness, bullying, middle school, and interpersonal skills.

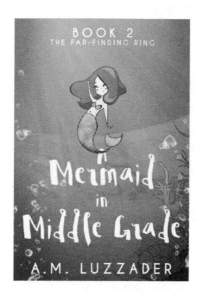

A Mermaid in Middle Grade: Book 2: The Far-Finding Ring

(Available now)

A young mermaid. False accusations. The dreadful sea witch. Can Brynn Finley navigate stormy waters to win back her best friend?

Jade Sands has been Brynn Finley's best friend since they were wee mer-babies. But when Jade's mother thinks Brynn has stolen her cherished pearls, she forbids the two mermaids to see one another. Determined to get her best friend back, Brynn sets out to find Phaedra the sea witch and solve the mystery of the missing jewelry. On her quest, Brynn makes new friends, learns new mer-magic, and discovers what it really means to be a friend.

Educational topics: Ocean and marine life, environmental conservation, bullying, friendship, mindfulness, and interpersonal skills.

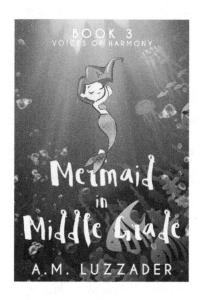

A Mermaid in Middle Grade: Book 3: Voices of Harmony

(Available now)

An unhealthy coral reef and pollution in the ocean. An entire undersea town turned upside-down. Can Brynn Finley solve Fulgent's latest mystery and get to the Jay Barracuda and the Killer Whales concert before Phaedra the sea witch turns her into a lowly sea slug?

When a beautiful and talented young mermaid named Priscilla Banks moves to Fulgent, everything starts going wrong for mermaid Brynn Finley. Her best friend ignores her, the sea witch is set free, and the seafolk of Fulgent are acting very strangely. As Brynn searches for clues, she learns a lot about friendship and settling differences, but time is running out—the sea witch has another dastardly and disgusting scheme to rid the oceans of humans. Soon the entire town is chasing Brynn, and her only friend is her trusty pet sea turtle!

The Mermaid in Middle Grade series is a middle-school fantasy adventure series of coming of age books appropriate for children ages 8–12 and all who enjoy middle grade books.

Educational topics: Ocean and marine life, environmental conservation, mindfulness, envy and jealousy, friendship problems, bullying, middle school, and interpersonal skills.

A Mermaid in Middle Grade: Book 4:
The Deep Sea Scrolls

Mermaid in Middle Grade: Book 5: The
Golden Trident

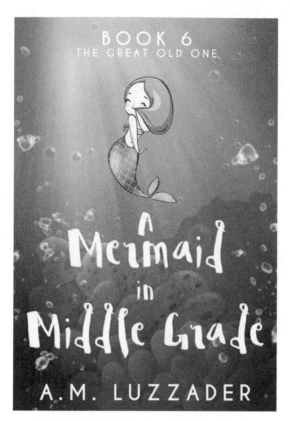

A Mermaid in Middle Grade: Book 6:
The Great Old One

Made in the USA
Las Vegas, NV
21 November 2021

34892469R00100